Honoring the Light in You

*Heart Opening Poems of Everyday Heroes, Yoga,
and Mind Body Spirit Wellbeing*

Julie Dunlop

Finishing Line Press
Georgetown, Kentucky

Honoring the Light in You

*Heart Opening Poems of Everyday Heroes, Yoga,
and Mind Body Spirit Wellbeing*

Copyright © 2022 by Julie Dunlop
ISBN 978-1-64662-941-1 First Edition
All rights reserved under International and Pan-American Copyright Conventions. No part of this book may be reproduced in any manner whatsoever without written permission from the publisher, except in the case of brief quotations embodied in critical articles and reviews.

Publisher: Leah Huete de Maines
Editor: Christen Kincaid
Cover Art and Illustrations: Benjavisa Ruangvaree Art/Shutterstock.com
Author Photo: Karen Dunlop
Cover Design: Elizabeth Maines McCleavy

Order online: www.finishinglinepress.com
also available on amazon.com

Author inquiries and mail orders:
Finishing Line Press
P. O. Box 1626
Georgetown, Kentucky 40324
U. S. A.

Table of Contents

The Cuckoo Clock Repair Shop 1
The Plant Waterer Who Speaks Six Languages 2
The Dazzles of Their "Fine" 3
The Gentlest Arrow 4
The Groomer Who Was Once a Cat 5
Fermata 6
The Cartographer Who Got Lost 7
In the Hovering Time of Not-Yet 8
Circuitry Within 9
Swimming Without Swimming 10
The Slowest Hour 12
Not Yet Tamed into Words 13
Wordless Prayers 15
Amidst the Ever-Swirling Spin 17
Unplugging 18
A Circus of New Platter Options 19
At the Carnival of Humanity 20
The Roots of Things 21
From Every Moment's Space 22
Wisps of Blue 23
Choreography of Stillness 25
The Judge Who Can (and Cannot) Decide 26
Feasting on Silence 28
Letting the Sludge of the Day Release 29
Odd Stars in the Pre-Dawn Quiet 30
Seed Sounds 32
Stronger Than Concrete and Lighter Than Air 34
Bowing to the Trees 35
Breathing out the Cobwebs 37
Cleaning the Seen and Unseen 38
Where Motors Hum 40
Untangling the Chains 41
Singing Past Any Logic 42
Death-in-Life 43

First Day on the Job	44
The Mask Maker	45
The Tripled Tempo	46
Avalanche of Anxiety	47
The Unsolved Case	48
Small Globes	50
The Musical Mazes of His Voice	51
The Emergency Switch	52
The Peace of Mind Shop	53
The Toy Maker	55
In the Dissonance	56
Catapulted to Stardom	57
The Competitive Blood	58
The Drive-Thru	60
On Call	61
In This Wild Market	62
Shifts and More Shifts	63
Spanning the Gap	64
70 Hours Per Week	65
Ocean of Intuition	66
Inside the Gaping Unknown	67
Lunar Luminosity	68
It Didn't Add Up	70
His Plan to Save the World	71
The Diamond of Lentils	72
Salutations to the Light	73
Witnessing the World	74
With Compassion	75
Reverse Ransom	76
Hungry for Normalcy	77
The Acrobat	78
A Living Temple	79
The Virtual Realm	80
The Frequent Flyer	81
A Continual Surrendering	83
Proud as a Peacock	84
Becoming Incandescent	85

Being a Student 86
The Intricacy of This Life 87
On Stage 88
Third Month of Furlough 89
The Job Applicant 90
The Retiree 91
Night Shift 92
She Is Up 93
In the Flow 94
Perhaps It Was the Shadow 95
The Dog Walker 96
The Ladder of the Spine 97
Searching the Crevices 98
The Bliss of Being Utterly Carefree 99
On the Open Sea 101
The Shared Fabric of Humanity 103
Making an Ogre Smile 105
She Thought She'd Seen It All 107
Between a Rock and a Hard Place 108
The Pastry Chef 110
The Page of This Day 111
The Woman with the Mismatched Earrings 113
On Another Planet 114
A Dream Job 115
The Butcher Who Lost His Flow 116
The Tantrum of Her Mind 117
The Aloe Vera Shop Employee 118
The Warehouse Manager 119
In the Stillness 121
Sirens of Fear 122
With the Economy Like It Was 123
The Green Song of Faith 124
The Dragon Maker 125
Polynomials Popping into Her Mind 126
In These Quiet Hours 127
On the Cusp 128
Opening to the Heavens 129

Miles Logged and Fares Accrued 130
Drifting Beyond Celsius, Fahrenheit 131
The Allergist Who Was Allergic 133
The Tattoo Artist.. 134
Cages Dissolving.. 136
Ten Tiny Shields of Color... 137
Blue Tulips with Forsythia.. 138
The Eraser Maker 139
The Xylophone Shop Musician.. 141
Newly Ripe 143
Galloping 144
A Potential Hiccup 145
In the Conference Room 147
In the Sweetness of Pre-Dawn 148
The Marshmallow Shop... 149
Eyes and Ears Alert 151
The Shoeshiner.. 152
The Sky Ablaze.. 154
Divinely Designed Lungs 156
Masking Her Shock 159
Beyond Coupons 161
Into the Beehive 162
Inside a Pocket of a Sci-Fi Film.. 164
The Unthinkable Backbend of Sky's Deep Blue......................... 166
The Frazzled Hairstylist 167
As the Colors Bloomed 168
Excavating 169
The Perfection of Imperfection... 170
The Unemployment Agency 171
Vast Cosmos.. 172
The Collective Sanctuary 173
Silent Victory 174
The Final Relaxation 175

❖ This symbol at the bottom of each page indicates the name of the yoga pose, technique, or concept that appears in the poem.

*This book is dedicated
with deep respect
to
all workers,
all retirees,
all who are studying and preparing for a career,
all who are changing careers or figuring out their career path,
all who are currently furloughed or unemployed,
and all who are engaged in the daily essential work of being human
~~
We are each essential in the shared continuum of life*

Dear Reader,

It is with deep gratitude that I offer these poems to honor the work—seen and unseen—performed by individuals across the country and around the world. The long hours, the long shifts, the expertise, the dedication: all of this is vital to our collective community and is so deeply appreciated.

Each job/career is sacred with its own purpose, its gifts, and its challenges, each day delivering something new. While this collection would be exponentially longer if it depicted every single profession, job, *āsana,* and aspect of yoga and wellbeing as a whole, I followed the flow of what was arriving to create a glimpse of the diverse and amazing individuals who are part of our collective community—and to honor the tremendous light that exists within us an individuals and in our shared humanity. The poems are also an exploration of the illumination of the practices of yoga that bless us in so many different ways: nourishing our health, supporting balance of mind-body-spirit, offering relief from stress, and so much more.

Meeting the challenges of daily life has become increasingly difficult during the pandemic. With rising levels of stress impacting mind-body-spirit wellbeing, simply showing up and being present for each moment at work and in daily living has taken on, in many cases, a heroic quality. In the midst of ongoing deep respect and appreciation for those who are literally saving lives and all of the essential workers who have shown up daily with great courage and dedication, let us also respect and appreciate the presence and contribution of each and every individual. With awareness of our diverse experiences in life, may we offer, as well, respect and compassion for those dealing with struggles, addictions, traumas, and losses who are making courageous decisions for positive transformation. As we, as individuals and as a national and global community, navigate immense internal and external challenges exacerbated by the pandemic, let us remember our shared humanity, the wisdom of self-care, and the vital ongoing journey of mind-body-spirit wellbeing.

In this collection of poems, the characters and situations are fictional. As such, please note that the poems do not constitute medical advice in any way. As always, check with your healthcare provider regarding any medical questions or concerns. To honor the wellbeing of mind, body, and spirit, please consult with your healthcare provider before beginning a yoga practice, and work with the guidance of a yoga teacher when learning yoga, such as *āsana* (yoga postures), *prāṇāyāma* (breathwork), etc. Thank you!

May these poems be an oasis for you in the midst of whatever stress exists in your life right now, and may health and harmony flourish!

Thank you so much for the gift of your presence and the sacred witness you are to the many exquisite and often perplexing layers of this life.

Remember the light within you, always!

The Cuckoo Clock Repair Shop

The woman who worked in the cuckoo clock
repair shop lived for 12:00 noon
when all of the tiny doors flew open
and the wooden birds sang,
their carved beaks filling the store
with their song. This was her anchor
in the sea of jaded customers asking,
"How much for the digital?" as if they'd rather
replace the clock than repair its aphasia.

Sometimes instead of losing their song,
the cuckoos called out at the wrong time,
startling their owners at twenty-three past.

When she found herself particularly stuck
on a repair like this, she put down her tools
and stood on one leg, wrapping the other leg
around it. She then wrapped one arm around the other
and crouched down, looking at the wounded clock,
her gaze sharpening like an eagle's, until there it came:
    the pathway into the repair.

In moments like this,
    she seemed to grow wings,
and at the base of her throat
    a tiny door popped open,
        a brightly plumed song releasing.

            ❖ *Garuḍāsana* (Eagle Pose)

The Plant Waterer Who Speaks Six Languages

The plant waterer who speaks six languages
could not fully translate the pleasure
she received from conversing with the plants
she watered in the upscale homes and offices
of the suburbs. It was not so much
what she said to them but what they said to her,
murmuring in their native languages,
fresh insights rolling from their leaf-like tongues.

Her employers, busy as they were, never stopped
to consider the fact that she might be fluent
in French, Arabic, Greek, Mandarin, or Spanish,
as well as English, any more than they wondered
about their plants' moods. A nod. A payment
quickly rendered, or perhaps a "Hi, how are you?"
if business was slow. That was okay. Better to sink
into the silence flowering with so many unexpected sounds
apparently only she could hear. The ferns, especially chatty,
she lingered with as long as possible, soaking in
their dialect rich with the syntax of ancient times.
Why she wasn't employed by the U.N. or a top ten
they could completely understand, knowing the lure
of decoding the text of what reaches beyond words,
the expanse of the cosmos within the breath.

Later, in the depths of night, she would stand, press her back
   against a quiet wall and tilt, keeping her body parallel
with the wall, lifting her back leg to a ninety-degree angle,
   stretching the lower arm downward against the wall
while reaching the other arm up to the sky,
   resting in the in-between like a half-moon
somewhere between light and night,
     between understand and understood

       ❖ *Ardha-Candrāsana* (Half-Moon Pose)

The Dazzles of Their "Fine"

The bank teller rode her smile like a sled
   over the icy tone of the customer
frustrated by the twenty-minute wait.
   Noticing the fiery pigment of his face,
she wanted to warn him about the cardiac strain
   of impatience, worry, regret.

Instead, she answered his questions
   about annuities while wondering what type
of mugs lined his cupboard. Would they be expensive
   like his vocabulary laden with Latinate terms?
Did he go home to rooms of rarely-walked-upon
   lavish rugs? The calculation of dollars and cents
required close attention, sidelining her desire
   to search for the relic in each customer's past
shading the tone of "Fine" when she asked how they were.

But that didn't stop her from noticing
   the discrepancies between customers'
bank account balances and the dazzles of their "Fine."
   Which voices gleamed like silver?
Which eyes shone like newly minted coins?
   She took note of these details
along with the amount of the deposit
   or withdrawal. And she hatched her theories.

But once five o'clock came, she was out of there,
   exchanging her high heels for bare feet,
sitting in front of her TV watching CNN.
   Extending her legs into a wide angle, she leaned
forward, grasping the outside edges of her feet
   with her hands, and straightening her back,
she suddenly felt she could fly,
   her outstretched legs and arms becoming two wings
gliding above all of the tragedies reported on the news,
   soaring beyond all buildings, all need for notaries or ATM's,
coasting gently on the upsurge of air flowing from her very own breath.

      ❖ *Upaviṣṭa-Koṇāsana* (Wide-Angled Seated Forward Fold)

The Gentlest Arrow

The professional oboist was ready to take the stage once more,
joining the other members of the woodwind quartet
that had been her bread and butter
for the past twelve years. Out of habit, she touched
her left pocket, checking for an emergency reed.
It was there. In all these years, she'd only needed it
twice. Would tonight be the third?

After hundreds of performances, she still felt jitters
in the furthest reaches of her veins, a slight
fluttering like thousands of tiny blue butterflies.
But once she entered into the hollow swells
of the sound her oboe made when she offered
it breath, she would not return until the last note
slipped into place.
    In that momentary pause
before the clapping began,
she would feel the presence
of the flutist, clarinetist, and bassoonist
and enter back into her own body, rich
with the colors the music had carried.

Only the aching in her fingers and wrists
confirmed the terrain she had travelled.
That, and the audience rising from their seats
in thunderous applause.
    In that awareness
of all attention focused on her, the lights
grew heavy and she wanted nothing more
than to flatten her stomach against the cool earth
and bend her knees, facing her soles to the stars,
wrapping her hands around her ankles,
lifting her knees, head, and chest, becoming in that moment
a bow from which the gentlest arrow of silence might sing.

           ❖ *Dhanurāsana* (Bow Pose)

The Groomer Who Was Once a Cat

The groomer who was once a cat
    sometimes catches himself licking his fingers
or smoothing away long whiskers no one else can see.
    When he brushes his long hair, he sometimes begins to purr.

"How come none of these cats claw you?" his scratched co-workers
    will ask. He just shrugs. Aloof. That's the word he overheard
someone using once to describe him. It would likely be impolite
    to explain how he prefers a warm patch of sunlight
to chit chat circling in on itself like the hands of a clock.

Eight hours on his feet clipping and trimming and scrubbing
    and soothing has worn him out. His back, with its mighty tantrums,
reminds him that he is no longer twenty-three, or forty-three.

As soon as he gets home and takes off his shoes,
    he plants his palms softly into the pale orange carpet
and, balancing on his hands and knees,
    he begins rolling his spine from his tailbone to his shoulder blades,
rounding his back so that his spine rises up to the moon,
    chin and tailbone tucked—before slowly moving
    his belly toward the earth, arching his back, lifting his head
and tailbone, his arms still at a full stretch, palms (paws) to the ground.
    Repeating this motion, breathing in and out in an even rhythm,
his body slowly flowing into something beyond two-legged
    or four-legged, purring.

    ❖ *Marjaryāsana/Bitilāsana* (Cat/Cow Pose)

Fermata

Tuxedo-tailed and baton in hand, the conductor jabs the air,
    the point of his baton piercing the pulsing.
      His hands pull flocks of purple-feathered birds
from hidden trees, stir up high winds pushing across
    fenceless fields, erase worlds with a motion,
coax animals to come close and let their voices rip.
    Any second he could become airborne
or topple off his platform—

Is his heart strong? So close to so many realities revolving
    and landscapes transforming so rapidly,
        the tempo of his dancing arms soars!

    Does he see flutes, tubas, and bassoons—or the cavalry
rushing toward him, fleets of ancient boats sails full,
    a jungle undone by panthers' claws?

The bows shoot up and down.
    An army of violins marches under the spell
of its leader, eyes wild with reports
    of forces approaching at uneven intervals,
      racing, faster, the crescendo of inevitable finale,

after which he will remove his coat and cummerbund,
    untuck his shirt, take off his shoes, and rest on his back
with his feet lifted, knees bent, hugging them into his chest,
    making himself round and compact—a steady whole note
in the midst of the background music of his mind,
    a fermata extending the hold,
slowing the rhythm
  of
his
  abundantly
harmonic
  breath.

      ❖ *Pavanamuktāsana/Apānāsana* (Knees-to-Chest Pose)

The Cartographer Who Got Lost

The cartographer who got lost
   in her own thoughts often looked up
only to realize she had no idea
   where she was, her feet traveling
in a different direction than her mind,
   the terrain of the past overlaid
with the imagined territory of the future
   making it impossible to chart
longitude or latitude, the landscape bending
   beyond the most precise navigational device.

To map the tributaries of her thoughts
   feeding the vast and often agitated sea
of consciousness would tax her skills,
   practiced though she was from nearly three decades
of translating the textures of the world.

Taming the mind was a completely different story.
   Incorrigibly, her attention refused to stabilize
into a sturdy mesa or even a coastal plain.

Defeated, she bent forward, loose and limp
   as a rag doll.
Then, reaching further, she touched
   the floor, placing the palms of her hands
in contact with the soles of her feet
   making a loop of herself, stopping her feet
from taking another step,
   and in doing so,
 quieting
   the incessant scouting
of her mind.

      ❖ *Pādahastāsana* (Forward Fold with Hands Beneath Feet)

In the Hovering Time of Not-Yet

Whenever the flight attendant felt the swerving
    of weather-induced turbulence, he said a prayer
while clinging to the statistic that more people die
    in automobile wrecks than in plane crashes.

    Then, visiting the sparsely populated terrace
of his heart, he would bring to mind the faces of loved ones.
    Simultaneously, he walked the narrow aisle
flashing a glossy smile to nervous passengers,
    assuring them that everything was under control.

The deer in the mountains below heard
    only the faintest hum in the sky and knew nothing
of the fear coursing through the veins of the flight attendant,
    the pilot, or any of the passengers.

    The waves
along the coast continued to flatten into foam
    and roll back into the sea, their rhythm unchanged
by anything overhead,
    except the moon.

Thousands of miles away, the flight attendant's cat
    cleaned its paws meticulously, paused, looked up,
and then returned to scrubbing its fur,
    at which time the flight attendant looked down
at his watch again,
    then looked up,
      waiting for the "fasten seatbelt" sign
to unblink.

In the hovering time of not-yet, he visualized himself kneeling,
    his legs tucked beneath him on a floor that was not airborne—
his thighs heroically pressing down into his calves,
    his spine strong and unwavering, his mind free
from visions of crash landings, his gaze calm
    and focused,
simultaneously relaxed
    and alert.

❖ *Virāsana* (Hero Pose)

Circuitry Within

The interpreter was unusually deft
at discerning the essences of a message
and finding a way to loop words
in another language together
to create a similar concept.
   For this reason,
and the fact that he typically dressed
in a three-piece suit, he was called upon
at all hours to ease the stampede
of unfamiliar languages and words.

If someone were to x-ray his translation
and compare it to the film of the original,
there would be discrepancies. Cereal
on the one hand, sausage and eggs on the other.
However, both were breakfast, and that was that.

Simple terms like *tree* and *table*
he worshipped, but not in the way he cherished
the challenges of translating *sacrum*
or the infinitely complex *lunar*.

   Most days, though,
his work took him to the lexicons of court proceedings,
financial transactions, and governmental contracts.
The neurons fired so quickly under such fast-paced
and high-stakes assignments that by the end
of the day he was mind-weary and ready to move
into a wordless space.

   Crossing his arms behind his back
and placing his feet wide apart,
he hinged at the hips, leveling down
with a flat back, gently releasing
his hands and head toward the ground,
all the word-shaped thoughts
of the day washed clean by the reverse
flow of the circuitry within.

❖ *Prasārita Pādottānāsana* (Wide-Legged Forward Fold)

Swimming Without Swimming

The oceanographer who couldn't swim
lived vicariously as he observed the undulations
   of the jellyfish tentacles, the quick darts
of the fish, the rippling of the wake
   of sea creatures making their way through the waves.

It wasn't that he hadn't tried. Six times
   he had signed up for swim lessons, and six times
he had not shown up, stomach aches and panic attacks
   emerging just at the thought of being submerged
without gills or fins.
   Maybe he had drowned in a prior life
he told himself for lack of a better way to explain his fear.

As he charted tides and recorded sonar frequencies,
   he could almost remember why the water overwhelmed him,
but just as soon as he moved close enough to touch
   the ever-receding past, it slipped away, churned back
out to the sea.
   He picked up the conch shell
that sat on his desk and cradled it to his ear
   like a cell phone, the rushing of the waves greeting him
     like a lifelong friend.
   Then he fingered the red coral
brought to him from the depths by a scuba diving colleague,
   his fingers drinking in the rough texture, the knobby angularity
of its underwater design.
   Next, he put on goggles
and flippers, moving apart the air with his dry hands.
   And in these waterless swims, he felt free from being
landlocked, being run ashore by his own fear.

   But when summer came and his fears splashed up in his face
mercilessly for months on end, there seemed to be
  only one way to find peace: to lie on his back
on the turquoise carpet and prop himself up on his elbows,
   arching his spine so that the top of his head
  rested gently against the blue.

With his chest opening
and his breath slowing, he began to shimmer
almost as if he had gills,
glimmering.

❖ *Matsyāsana* (Fish Pose)

The Slowest Hour

The gas station clerk stood inside the small rectangle of space
   behind the cash register watching the hours click by.
     I'm vital, he reassured himself as he rang up
customers' purchases of caffeine: super-sized coffees,
   ice cold Mountain Dews, Red Bull, Pepsi, Coke, you name it.
This fuel, they believed, was every bit as important as the fuel
   flowing into the metal mouths of the vehicles
parked outside at the pump.

   And then there were the lottery fanatics.
They were crazed enough as it was
   with their very special choices of numbers,
combinations they were sure would unlock
   the prosperity of their future. Good luck, he told each one,
sending them out into the world on a ray of hope.

Off they went on their journeys, as close
   as across the street or as far as across the state
and beyond, the cross-country travelers road-weary
   and lonesome for a voice not coming from the radio
or through a cellphone. He knew the feeling.

He called it "The 3 a.m. Black Hole," the slowest hour
   in his graveyard shift. The partiers had passed out
by then and the early risers were not yet in pursuit
   of their morning paper, coffee, and donut.
     During these lulls,
when he struggled to stay awake, he sometimes stood
   in front of the display of small bags of chips
with his legs wide apart, bending his front knee, lowering
   his hips and torso while extending his arms wide
shoulder height and parallel to the ground.
   Directing his gaze
to his front hand,
   he felt his strength gathering
     as if he were invincible, a warrior armed
   with the hidden laser
of a most keenly focused breath.

❖ *Vīrabhadrāsana II* (Warrior 2 Pose)

Not Yet Tamed into Words

The Shop of Words originated from the twin languages
   of despair and innovation,
both of which the proprietor of the shop was fluent in.

As an etymologist, he had found
   that tracing the long, winding history
of a word was not unlike genetic research,
   the subtleties of linguistic telomeres
hinting at the word's lifespan.
   He had also learned,
mostly through trial and error, how much to share
   of his arcane knowledge. As soon as fog set in
across the face of a customer,
   he would gently shift gears, inviting him or her
to continue browsing.
   Even without anomia,
his customers often could not find
   what they wanted. Sometimes they stayed so long
and asked so many questions he was tempted
   to send them home with a complimentary thesaurus.
But that would have been like offering carryout fast food
   to one who considers eating an art and savors
the ambiance of a fine restaurant as much as the meal.

Maybe he was just losing his patience
   after one too many inquiries like "What's a good word
to describe that feeling when you know
   you've turned off your cell phone before going to a funeral
but you're still afraid it might ring?"

At times like these when he was unsure how to proceed,
   he excused himself through the purple curtains
to the back of the shop where he knelt on the floor,
   gazed to the center of his forehead,
and opened his mouth so wide that his tongue spilled free,
   a roar of breath erupting from deep within.
A few more roars and he was good to go,
   rising up on his haunches,

striding confidently once more
    through the jungle
of what has not yet been tamed
    into words.

❖ *Siṃhāsana* (Lion Pose)

Wordless Prayers

The gallery owner swore there was a phantom
   who nudged visitors when they lingered too long
in front of certain paintings.
      The large oil painting,
for instance, seemed to brighten the sunken faces
   of tired tourists who had seen more art that day
than in their entire lives.
      But nearly as soon as they formed a semicircle
around the painting, they moved on—
   as if propelled by the dynamic voice of a preacher at a revival.

No one had bought a painting in weeks
   and the heavy framed canvases
felt like logs pressing down
   on the gallery owner's lungs.
How could she redeem her promises
   that the art placed in her gallery would sell?

As the metal edges of "always" began to corrode,
   she made a silent bargain with the phantom:
If you allow visitors to linger, I'll leave you
   a peace offering each and every morning.

Each night at home after work, she lit candles
   as she selected from a palette of poses,
creating a wide range of shapes with her body.
   Gradually, the worries of the day
faded from neon to pastel,
   and she offered her wordless prayers:
hinging forward at the hips from a standing position,
   reaching her arms out straight ahead, pressing her hands
into the wall, looking down, keeping her back parallel to the floor.
   Holding this position, she became
a corner of one of the framed paintings in the gallery.

Then, recreating this angle on the floor by sitting with an upright spine,
   palms pressing into the floor by her sides,
legs extended in front, feet flexed,

  she became another corner framing a new painting
coming into view in her mind's eye
  with the brush stroke
of each revitalizing breath.

     ❖ *Daṇḍāsana* (Staff Pose)

Amidst the Ever-Swirling Spin

The man at the ketchup factory
   sees red—eight hours a day
and then again in his sleep,
   his dreams colored by crimson
rhythms, odd images drifting past
   on the conveyor belts of his mind,
the plastic containers of time
   filling, one by one, capped
with quick-fitting words of light.

Eight years from retirement
   and many mortgage payments to go,
he clocks in, clocks out, clocks in
   and again the weeks slog by,
churning the months
   and graying his hair.
     Somewhere
a glob of ketchup is accompanying
   an order of fries, dressing up
a freshly grilled burger or a veggie hot dog.

   Somewhere there is a redless quiet
beyond the whirring machinery.

As the bottles of ketchup glide by
   hundreds at a time, he stands,
breathing: the four corners of his feet
   pressing into the factory floor.
     Unlocking
his knees. Aligning his shoulders
   and hips.
     Amidst the ever-swirling spin
of all that will not relent, he becomes,
   if only for a few moments,
 a mountain,
     unshakeable,
absolutely
   serene.

❖ *Tāḍāsana* (Mountain Pose)

Unplugging

The cable repairman had heard rumors
  about this house. Things about silvery shag carpet,
figurines of frogs—hundreds of them—
  and couches as soft as magnolia petals.

As the reverberation of the doorbell went spinning
  into the inner chambers of the house,
he stared at the bark on the sculpted shrub
  by the door, wondering if this job was worth the risks.

Daily, he went out of the frying pan—the office—
  and into the fire. Yes, there was the occasional offer
of lemonade or coffee, but more often shreds of patience
  flew in a mad confetti. Taking away
some people's cable was like depleting their oxygen.

As they pummeled him with questions
  of "How much longer?" and the like, he summoned
the scent of fresh cedar and breathed deeply.
  This approach kept him going until he could complete
his repairs and head home to his own modems and screens
  where he had his choice of endless channels.

Opting for silence, he stretched himself out like a long cable,
    propping himself up on his right elbow,
balancing on his right side, his head cradled in his right hand.
    Then, lifting his left leg up to the sky,
he looped his left thumb and first finger around his left big toe,
    creating a right angle between his lifted leg and lower leg.
        As he held this pose, he traveled
farther and farther away
    from the anxiety of his customers,
        unplugging
from the stresses of the day,
    connecting slowly with his breath,
recharging the dynamo of his soul.

❖ *Anantāsana* (Side Reclining Leg Lift Pose)

A Circus of New Platter Options

The caterer often woke up in the middle of the night
   inspired by the possibilities of food imitating art.
His most recent epiphany: turtle shells out of cantaloupe rinds.
   A circus of new platter options spun his mind with pewter shine.

Sleep was a bucket he could not pour himself into,
   not with a fantasy of applause urging him to design
a kaleidoscope image with slivers of orange, kiwi, and pineapple.

The clock blinked back at him. 2 a.m. would qualify
   as a snack time, he decided. He piled up pieces of dry cereal
in different designs, imagining making the great pyramids
   of Egypt out of cubes of cheese. That just might work
for happy hour, he said to his wide-eyed cat, thinking
   of upscale tavern-like business gatherings.

If only he could figure out something exciting to do
   with filtered water. The grandfather clock with the face
of a gourmet pizza chimed 3 and the caterer, realizing the need
   to attempt some more shut-eye before his day
of black-tie expectations, found the cufflinks of dawn.
   Moving to the pie-themed rug in the living room,
he rolled himself out on the floor.
   Bringing the soles of his feet
together and relaxing his knees toward the ground,
   he reached for a string of old neckties he had knotted together
and looped it around his waist, placing the band of neckties
   against his feet to help secure the position.

Reclining with a couch cushion under his back
   and a pillow beneath each knee, he was now ready to bake.
"Bake" is what he called the necessary wait time,
   or else he would never stay still.
"Raw dough" he often repeated to himself silently
   to help pass the time, to slow his mind.
And in the way a packet of yeast can make dough sing,
   these slow minutes on the floor restored him, transforming him,
gradually, into a soft loaf of sleep,
   deliciously content.

❖ *Supta-Baddha-Koṇāsana* (Reclined Bound Angle)

At the Carnival of Humanity

Here she is again, at the carnival of humanity,
   where she will padlock her opinions and only ask,
with the pinkest of voices, if a ma'am or sir would like hashbrowns
   or toast, regular or decaf, fried or scrambled.
The waitress is used to scraping herself out of bed
   on cold mornings before dawn and jumping into her lemon-colored outfit,
complete with stitched nametag. She still can't, however, get used to
   complete strangers inserting her name in their causal breakfast dialogue.
"Aurora, would you mind warming up my coffee?"
   Or "it sure is gonna be a beauty today, Aurora, now don't ya think?"
She presses her lips together in a tip-winning smile
   and builds a patio off the edge of her mind, bricked
with all the internal chatter her customers will never hear.

Later, she will go home and sit out on her balcony
   overlooking the sea. In the salt air breeze, she will sit
with her right foot nestled between her left thigh and left calf,
   and her left foot nestled between her right thigh and right calf,
her toes securely tucked into the shelter of her knees,
   the tamed toes calming her mind into a growing focus
on the rhythm of her in-breath and out-breath,
   quieting the echo of her customers' comments,
the inner waves of the breath as soothing
   as the waves she will hear faintly in the distance
as they make their way to shore
   before slowly washing back out to sea.

❖ *Svastikāsana* (Auspicious Pose)

The Roots of Things

The botanist's pockets were filled with petals, leaves,
   pinecones, and other pickings.
What he wanted to say
   when people asked him about his line of work
wrapped around his tongue
   like a morning-glory vine.

Other thoughts that he wanted to think
   remained dormant, curled inside winter's seed,
not yet able to unfurl.
   It was with the plants themselves
he communicated most fluently,
   the silent veins of their understanding expanding
 well beyond the radius
   of even the most river-wrung words.

How he had learned the language of leaves
   is something only the trees themselves knew,
tapping in as they do to the roots of things.

When he could not speak at all, the words
   refusing to flower, he balanced himself
carefully on the four corners of both feet,
   aligning his ankles, hips, and shoulders.
Then, sliding his left foot up to the top of his right leg
   and pressing the left sole into his right thigh,
his left knee pointing outward, he lifted his arms
   above his head, fingertips pointing to the sky,
his thoughts gently fluttering in a breeze
   slowly dying down.

          ❖ *Vṛkṣāsana* (Tree Pose)

From Every Moment's Space

The sonographer measured the tempo of his days
   by what he called pivots. Pivots were the points in time
right before he touched probe to skin
   and the window into another being's inner terrain
opened. He could not unknow what he knew
   after that moment. He could not unsee what he had seen.
Often, he paused to inhale and exhale slowly before beginning
   the scan of the kidneys, liver, and abdomen,
honoring the inner mysteries, the realm of the unknown.

The masses that revealed themselves were known
   to him first, before the individuals in whom they resided,
before the physicians who would clear their throats
   and say, "I'm afraid I have some bad news," before
the family members who would stumble and stagger
   momentarily before offering sunshiny words to ward off
the gray. And what about the shadows that would masquerade
   as potential masses creating tumbling spirals of needless stress
and futile appointments with doctors ordering follow-up tests,
   checking for something that wasn't there?
The bodies laid out like vibrant corpses
   reminded him, when he wasn't overbooked, of his own
susceptibility, of the way in which one cell's mutation
   separated him from the jagged face of mortality
staring back at him from every moment's space.

Sometimes, on particularly busy days, when he felt
   his energy flagging and his vision beginning to glaze,
he stepped into the break room and placed his palms and feet
   on the ground, pushing his hips into the air
so that his legs and arms formed an upside-down V,
   the inversion stirring the stagnant blood
and sending it circulating in such a way
   that when he walked his hands to his feet
he was able to stand up straight again and focus
   his attention with the precision of a laser.

❖ *Adho-Mukha-Śvānāsana* (Downward Dog Pose)

Wisps of Blue

The cotton candy maker estimated
   that she had spun over seven thousand spools
of fluffy blue sugar around the big metal vat
   and onto the white-paper-swirled sticks to sell.

It wasn't that she minded spending her days
   doing the same task over and over—
in fact, she rather enjoyed the reliable rhythm.

She had even gotten used to arriving at home
   each evening with little wisps of blue
threaded through her hair.
   It was more the way
people assumed that since she sold cotton candy
   she didn't understand things like trigonometry
and astronomy.
   She could see it in the way
they looked past her, or through her.

Still, that did not diminish the joy
   of seeing the smiles that spread across children's faces
 as they approached her stand. Sometimes,
   of course, the children were five or six feet tall
and wrinkled with decades of dilemmas.
   Businessmen, in their three-piece suits, even appeared
from time to time, sheepishly ordering a taste
   of their childhood.

On this downtown corner,
   far from any coast, she often swore she heard
seagulls or the sound of the surf
   spilling from a customer's seaside recollections.
All in all, it was a fair way to make a living—
   adding sweetness to cloudy, traffic-filled days.

Her legs and feet, however, had a different view.
   Standing, standing, and more standing.

But oh, how it helped to lie down,
    prop her hips up with her hands and extend her legs
skyward, allowing all of the complaints
    of her legs and feet to drain away, reversing
and renewing the flow of her day.

             ❖ *Sarvāṅgāsana* (Shoulder Stand Pose)

Choreography of Stillness

Whistling as the brisk morning air skimmed across his bearded face,
    the sanitation worker hung on the side of the truck
grinding its way through one neighborhood at a time.
    Taking things away,
gathering the unwanted items kicked out to the curb
    in the weekly ritual of purging, he sometimes
felt heavy, weighed down by the garbage
    as if he himself were the landfill teeming
with half-eaten yogurts, half-used notebooks,
    chipped mugs, and torn socks.
He tried to focus on the empty dumpsters
    he was leaving along the streets, their mouths
ready to receive the next week's batch of discards,
    the continuum of weekly cycles keeping the gears greased
and turning weeks into months into years.

Still, sometimes he felt as emptied out as these dumpsters—
    and when his shift ended, he headed straight home
to shower and change, the odor of soured milk
    mixed with rancid oil washing away more easily
than his despair.

Later, he went to his mat and began warming up
    for his favorite pose, one slow movement at a time.
Then, standing and steadying himself on his left leg,
    he bent his right knee, holding his right foot
with his right hand, drawing the right leg back and up.
    Leaning his torso forward
and lifting the sole of his right foot up to the sky,
    he extended his left arm out in front,
thumb and index finger touching,
    becoming, in that moment, a dancer,
the choreography of stillness freeing within him
    something sacred, unable to be purchased
or ever thrown away.

            ❖ *Naṭarājāsana* (Dancer Pose)

The Judge Who Can (and Cannot) Decide

The judge who can't decide which flavor of ice cream
    or which scent of laundry detergent to buy
and becomes paralyzed in front of the packaged salad display
    debating between arugula and spinach, iceberg lettuce and romaine,
has no trouble deciding a guilty or non-guilty verdict.

This same person who is perplexed by choosing wintermint, spearmint,
    fresh mint, or peppermint mouthwash can see clearly
into the alibis of the accused and discern with confidence
    which ones are legitimate.
Yet he can stand at the post office counter
    comparing the various styles of stamps so long
that the postal employee will have to prompt him:
    Sir, have you made your selection?
He is likewise stymied
    by choosing between sirloin and salmon at a business lunch
or between red wine and white wine at an evening meal.

Still, he had no trouble determining who was at fault
    in a court of law, slamming his gavel down with conviction.
It was only once in a great while that he, praised near and far
    for his discernment in the courtroom, became stumped
by a case. He felt his mind stutter to a halt,
    his whole being flummoxed
by contradictions and contortions of data and linguistics.
    The clarity he relied upon became quicksand, and his pride gasped
to see how quickly he could lose his footing. In the midst
    of such tribulation, he would take a recess from the trial
and retreat to his chambers.

Taking care to close the door behind him,
    he would enter the sanctity of his office,
remove his judicial robe and shoes,
    and kick his legs up into a handstand,
allowing the support of his arms and hands
    to hold him suspended in space,
the confusion rushing right out of him,
    so that when he returned to standing upright,

his mind was clear and calm
   as a windless lake.

❖ *Adho-Mukha-Vṛkṣāsana* (Handstand Pose)

Feasting on Silence

The telemarketer who started taking extra shifts
to help out his co-workers began hearing himself
speaking his own script
in the middle of his dreams, waking him
to the difficult truth that his soul
was slowly being strangled,
exasperating hours
of telephone calls wrapping him
like the cord of a landline.
     When he tried to call
his former self, he got a busy. If only
he could use Caller ID to identify the source
of the thoughts plaguing him like repeated
robocalls.
     It was not easy living between
extremes—people either hung up at the sound
of his voice, blasting him for interrupting their day,
or kept him on the line with endless questions
because they were so starved for conversation.
The actual sales were few and far between.

In nearby cubicles, the same script cycled through
   at varying paces in an array of accents,
dizzying the stale air with a collage of buzzing,
   as if an entire hive had been loosed.

It was no wonder that he often feasted on silence
   when he went home, enjoying the wordlessness
as he sat, stacking his knees one on top of the other,
   reaching his right arm up, bending the right elbow,
and sending his right hand to the top of his back.
   The left arm he then extended parallel to the ground,
thumb facing the floor. Bending his left elbow, he glided
   his left hand to the center of his spine,
letting it journey upward,
   meeting his right hand
like two sides of a conversation
   flowing in tandem,
joining together at heart center.

❖ *Gomukhāsana* (Cow-Face Pose)

Letting the Sludge of the Day Release

The plumber is tense. She is wavering
    between admitting that she cannot free
the strangled portion of the drain
    and hunkering down for a final attempt
that could damage the pipe altogether.

Putting aside the mask of pride, she decides
    to call it a day. She packs up her toolbox slowly,
like a world-class flautist
    putting away her instrument slowly
after encountering the first piece she cannot play on sight.

At home, she retreats to the quiet, sitting on the wood floor.
    She bends one knee, bringing that foot on top of the opposite thigh.
Then, lifting the other foot with her hand, she creates
    a mirror image so that each thigh now holds the foot
of the opposite leg.

 In this cross-legged position, she rests,
    letting the mud,
 sludge,
    and slime
of the day
    release
fully-formed white petals—
    the unmistakable bloom
        of peace.

            ❖ *Padmāsana* (Lotus Pose)

Odd Stars in the Pre-Dawn Quiet

Hair netted, hands gloved, he folds foil
   around breakfast burritos. They shine
like odd stars in the pre-dawn quiet.
   Soon, hands will reach for them,
later, for sandwiches, burgers, fries.
   By then, he will be ladling meatballs,
straining spaghetti, scooping mac and cheese.

He watches them as they enter the cafeteria,
   smelling the mix of aromas.
Their eyes widen as they see
   something that suggests it could fill
the hungers bellowing inside.

He knows those hungers and their cruel tricks,
   how they can birth cravings
for things that breed more hunger.

So now, at night, instead of reaching for a beer or nachos
   or heading to the casino, he stretches out on his back
on the floor of his apartment and listens to music,
   counting his breaths.

Once he reaches fifty, he bends his knees,
   props up his back with his hands,
     extending his legs, lifting them
in a straight line toward the sky,

and then, hinging at the waist, he sends his legs
   over his head slowly like a lever,
     his toe tips gently touching
the ground.
     In this position, he rests,
considering the kinds of thoughts
   he'd like to plant
in this freshly plowed silence
   teeming with all the potential
     of a richly composted soil

nourished
by the earth-warming light
   of the sun.

❖ *Halāsana* (Plow Pose)

Seed Sounds

The tall glass jars that lined the teal shelves
    were each labeled: cilantro, marigold, tomato,
and so on, all in alphabetical order.
    The flowers and vegetables-to-be sat humbly on display,
their white spheres, black commas, flat gray ovals
    seeming entirely incapable of transforming
into robust plants.
    Mixed in with the labeled jars of standard fare
of sunflower seeds and the seed pods of morning glories
    were others: silence, reconciliation, joy.

Inside these particular jars were tiny folded pieces of paper.
    And when customers brought the jars
they had chosen up to the counter for their seeds
    to be scooped, bagged, and weighed,
they were invited to reach into the jars
    and pull out one of the folded pieces.

What was on the paper one could not be sure,
    but there they came, back again, ready
to do more planting in the soil of their soul.
    There was one customer, in fact,
who arrived repeatedly with requests
    for new categories: curiosity, compassion, conflict resolution.
Today's request was no less challenging—liberation.

As the customers knew, at least a twenty-four-hour turnaround time
    was needed for a new request. Still, they stayed to browse:
Radishes. Resilience. Reverence. Romaine lettuce. Rutabaga.

The shop owner, who had lain dormant
    in retirement for eight years before opening the store,
blessed-cursed its success.
    When he found himself
overwhelmed to the point of wanting to knock the jars
    off an entire shelf, he retreated
to his office and shut the door.

As his assistant manned the front desk, he sat quietly
   on the ground in a crossed-leg position
      repeating a seed sound
until peace wrapped its gentle tendrils around him
   like a vine that just won't quit.

         ❖ *Japa* (Repetition of Mantra)

Stronger Than Concrete and Lighter Than Air

The construction worker left the concert early.
    He hated to walk away from the haunting melody
of the bassoon. It was so much more pleasing
    than the hypnotic sounds of machinery
that accompanied his days.
    No doubt he would be put on trial
by his co-workers in the morning with interrogations
    of why he hadn't shown up at the bar. It didn't matter.
He was getting better at avoiding the holes
    they tried to dig in his day. And besides,
what did they know about the way an oboe solo
    could climb into your soul?

He cleared his throat
    and searched for the button inside that his co-workers
tried to press—the one that said something was wrong
    with him. It was becoming more and more fuzzy
as he plunged deeper into the ocean of what he loved.
    The list was in the double digits and grew daily
as he hammered and measured. This list
    of what built his joy woke him at 5 a.m.
and pushed him through the daylong sun (or rain).
    It serenaded him as he released the weight of his tool belt.
It was stronger than concrete and lighter than air.

Removing his steel-tipped boots, he reclined upon the cement,
    softening his bones and muscles until the hardness of the cement
no longer distracted him. Extending his arms on the ground
    at shoulder level, he scooped his knees toward his chest.
To the right he pivoted, exhaling, directing his knees
    toward his right elbow. On an inhale, he drew
his bent legs back to center and then lowered them to the left
    on the exhalation. Repeating this movement slowly released his back
without fail. The heavy lifting, the expectations, the assumptions—
    all of this fell away in the smooth rhythm
of the slow metronome his tanned body had just become.

❖ *Jaṭhara Parivartanāsana* (Reclined Twist Pose)

Bowing to the Trees

The date grower who was afraid of heights
knew better than to mention his acrophobia
or to question his fate, to wonder which karmic seed
had planted the irony, the paradox that had become
his life. Instead, with a subtle subterfuge,
he hired a bevy of workers to scale the tall ladders
up into the large leaves of the palm trees
where the dates ripened, growing plump and juicy
in the sun.
            Each year, when the crop was ready
to be harvested, invariably one of the workers
would publicly offer him the opportunity to be the first
to climb and pluck the first date of the crop.
Feigning humility, he would politely refuse,
asking the worker to do the honors instead,
and the worker, pleased to have such a down-to-earth
boss, would oblige, beaming. And so it went,
year after year, no one ever guessing
his secret.
            Still, it gnawed on him in the depths of his quiet.
When the wind stirred up the air and rustled the leaves,
he felt them taunting him, reminding him of his fear.
His attention scattered. His breathing strained.
And somewhere amidst the internal chaos, a memory
appeared:
            He stood beneath the trees and stars
and moved his left foot forward.
Then, pressing his palms together
in prayer position behind his back,
he hinged at the hips,
lowering down with a flat back,
taking his nose down toward his left knee.
            He stayed like this for several minutes,
as if bowing to the trees. Then, slowly, he returned
to standing position and switched sides,
moving his right leg ahead and, with a flat back,
bowing forward once again. Why this helped
or why he could then walk back inside and drift
into a deep sweet sleep he could not begin to explain.

❖ *Pārśvottānāsana* (Pyramid Pose)

Breathing Out the Cobwebs

The kaleidoscope maker scouted nature for designs,
   locating patterns in the pinecones, the wings of butterflies,
rose blossoms, and even the insides of kiwi.

As he lay awake in pre-dawn hours,
   he watched the circle of his mind
configure and reconfigure a cleome,
   substituting its pastels with fluorescent colors,
rotating its wild design ninety degrees, spiraling it,
   breathing in the fragrance of success.

True kaleidoscope connoisseurs were a high-standards lot,
   not easily impressed or even amused.
So when he hit upon an idea that would please
   the ocular taste of the elite, something
within him came into sharper resolution,
   the pixels of his lungs becoming more vivid,
the molecules of air moving with greater ease.

But when he got stuck, as inevitably he did
   from time to time, he felt his world darken
into a deep, empty cave, the kind through which
   the wind moans on deserted cliffs
high in the mountains of distant lands.

In these rare slumps, it was only after
   several days of despair that he could pull himself up
into a standing position.
   Stepping one foot forward,
he bent his front knee into a lunge,
   both feet rooting firmly into the ground.
Raising his arms above his head, he looked straight ahead,
   a warrior staring into the abyss of uncertainty,
breathing out the cobwebs,
   breathing in the light.

❖ *Vīrabhadrāsana I* (Warrior 1 Pose)

Cleaning the Seen and Unseen

She checked the lock on the door to her duplex again
    before heading through the wavy quiet of dawn
to the bus stop. Her schedule was unchanging, like the bus's.
    This early morning ride was not unwelcome as she spun
her thoughts against the corners of this precious privacy
    like a spider.
        By the time the patterns of her thoughts
were just beginning to bloom,
    it was time to greet the neon vacancy sign
as she stepped onto the sidewalk in front of the place
    of musical rooms.
        Same rooms, different people—
changing—like the children's birthday party game with chairs.
    Oh, how the musics flickered in these rooms after the keys
had been turned in at check-out time. When she went in to clean,
    she felt them rubbing up against the quiet space.
Some rooms were positively soupy with unseen residue.
    Teenagers, no doubt, or large families fighting—
their homemade tunes of "it's your fault" and "leave me alone"
    were unmistakable.
        When she had tried to ask her supervisor
about these messes and what she should do with them,
    he had spoken with words brittle as dry spaghetti,
accusing her of trying to cheat him into paying her more
    to clean invisible messes.
        After she had dried her tears,
she found that if she opened the window a few inches
    and said a prayer, these scattered songs eventually drifted away.
Her frustrations, too, began to fade once she was back
    in the comfort of her own clutter, her uniform neatly hung.
In the softness of a sweatsuit, she sat down on the carpet
    of her own room and stretched her right leg out in front of her,
bending her left knee and pressing the sole of her left foot into the floor.
    Turning toward the bent knee, she wrapped her right arm
around her left knee, hugging it close.
    As her left hand pressed into the floor, she turned her head
to look over her left shoulder, the flow of her breath

vacuuming out her lungs, her veins,
the long, labyrinthine hallways of her mind.

❖ *Ardha Matsyendrāsana* (Half-Fish Pose, variation)

Where Motors Hum

Behind the silvery foil of congratulations
   was the staggering truth: he was now married.
It was like an entire car had landed squarely on the mechanic's head.
   He had known for months that he was getting married
but somehow the excitement had chained up the details
   of what this would actually mean. No quarrel could make him stop
loving his wife or wanting to be with her. It wasn't that.
   It was more like an inability to grasp how this engine of daily togetherness
worked. He felt like someone drawn into a cartoon, unable to read the caption.
   For the first time, the idea of writing a letter to an advice columnist
crossed his mind. He watched it cross. He would never do that.
   What has he thinking? His job was fixing things, for crying out loud!
He moved his razor slowly over his chin, as if a clean shave
   might mean the strange feeling in his heart would disappear,
and his stumbling in this new dimension would fall, brush itself off,
   and walk into the place where motors hum.

Who was he kidding? He was massively stressed out.
   He blasted his music. Ten minutes until he needed to go
to work. There was time: he lowered himself down to the floor
   in plank pose, and lifting his left hand off the ground,
he turned his torso to the left.
   Crossing the left foot in front of his right,
      he propped himself up
by his right arm and hand and the edges of his feet.
   Extending his left arm up to the sky,
he felt the strength of his own body surge within
   as if he could support an entire vehicle with one hand.
He stayed here for five breaths—gliding into a plank position
   before turning slowly to the right,
balancing on his left hand and the edges of his feet,
   right arm saluting the sky,
his body a dynamic diagonal line of energy
   charging up his battery, energizing him
to travel bravely into the challenges of the day ahead.

        ❖ *Vasiṣṭhāsana* (Side Plank Pose)

Untangling the Chains

The jeweler disenchanted by her own designs
   believed success to be something glinting in the distance,
something just out of reach, beyond the next earring
   she crafted out of silver, beyond the next pendant
she made from topaz or glass, beyond the next pattern
   she conceived for a beaded bracelet,
beyond anything that she could bring into the universe
   to adorn a wrist, a neck, an ankle, an earlobe,
a finger.

     The rings she made were prized
by those delighting in intricacy and simplicity
   woven together with grace. Her designs garnered
praise and awards, pulling in buyers from across the globe.
   Still, she remained divorced from her own art,
seeing it as light years away from what she was sent
   to this planet to do.

     What this mission was exactly,
however, remained unclear, and she was constantly working
   to unknot it as if it were a tightly tangled chain
of finely spun gold. But sometimes these very efforts
   only succeeded in further tangling, one thought
knotting into the next. How could she breathe freely
   when her mind was so bound up?
She sighed, and sat down cross-legged.

     Turning to the right,
she took her left hand to her right knee,
    placing her right hand on the floor behind her right hip,
  and turned to look over her right shoulder.
Then, untwisting herself,
   she paused, and turned to the left,
     with her right hand on her left knee.
   In a way that she couldn't quite put into words,
these simple movements seemed to help, much more
    than the complex designs of her thoughts,
      shining though they were.

        ❖ *Parivṛtta-Sukhāsana* (Gentle Seated Twist)

Singing Past Any Logic

The mortician heard a violin's slow ache
    each time he gazed at another pair of closed eyes.
The horizontal posture of the people
    with whom he spent his days was affecting
his perspective increasingly as an accent
    becomes stronger the longer one lives in a place.
Learning details about the people he worked on
    became small ornaments in his day,
like this one fought in the war, or this one
    lost his life in a hot air balloon. These scraps
of information made them more than anatomy,
    more than knuckles, knees, and noses.
The scent of cigarette smoke on a suit coat
    would wake up an image of an earlier time,
when the soul of the embalmed could laugh out loud.

The mortician returned home
    after days like this in a quiet green glow.
At dinner, he noticed the gleam in the silverware,
    the texture of the napkin, the full circle of the plate before him.
And after the meal had been digested, the dog walked,
    the news watched, and emails returned, he would drop gently
to his knees, extending one leg out to the side.
    Balancing on one knee and on the opposite heel,
he lifted his arms to the sky, and with palms facing each other,
    he leaned over toward the extended leg,
keeping his hips and shoulders facing forward.
    Breathing into his abdomen, he could feel a tightness
not yet ready to release.
    When he returned to center
and repeated the stretch on the opposite side,
    he noticed the tightness beginning to ease
ever so slightly,
    his breath flowing deeply,
an internal balance emerging, singing past
    any earthly logic, any external correlation.

        ❖ *Parīghāsana* (Gate Pose)

Death-in-Life

The groundskeeper edged his mower carefully
around the corners of the markers,
glancing now and then at the names
on the granite faces, calculating the lifespan,
conjuring an image of Sylvia or Curtis
or whatever name had been engraved
letter by letter into the stone
to perch on the earth and glimmer
in the sun, to receive offerings of flowers
and whispered words.

The markers remaining unvisited year after year
he cleaned most carefully, pivoting
at each right angle with military precision.

It was only when he had put the mower away,
buried his head beneath a cool shower,
and laid down to rest that he found himself
on his back, legs apart and arms ever so slightly
angled away from his body, his eyelids
gently closed, his very soft breathing
dropping him deeper—moment by moment—
into the death-in-life relaxation of a corpse.

❖ *Śavāsana* (Corpse Pose)

First Day on the Job

As he sat inside his car trying to compose himself,
   through his mind flew a plane with the banner:
"You don't get a second chance to make a first impression."
   He watched the words billow and ripple.

After a long hiatus from work, he was more than ready
   to start earning a paycheck, but the thought
of all the staff members to meet and all of the new policies to learn
   had him nearly paralyzed, as well as his fear of not being able
to keep up with the demands of his new position.

Even as he was outwardly paralyzed, inside his nerves
   were on overdrive. He watched the clock,
gauging the last possible minute he could exit his car
   and still make it inside on time.

He would definitely go to yoga that night, he thought,
   and the mere thought of relaxing took his anxiety level
down a notch. "When you're afraid of losing your balance,"
   his yoga teacher would say, "find a *dṛṣṭi*, a gazing point
on the wall or the floor to help steady you."

He wondered if this would work now, in modified form,
   and desperate for support, he began focusing on a symbol of peace
in his mind's eye, letting his mind center on that one syllable: *peace*.

When it was time to go in,
   he opened the car door,
keeping his focus steady,
   as ready now as he would ever be
to face, to embrace
   whatever awaited him inside.

        ❖ *Dṛṣṭi* (Gazing Point)

The Mask Maker

By candlelight, he sat at his sewing machine
    soothed by its rhythm, watching stitches appear
in the colorful materials left over
    from costumes he'd designed from Broadway
through the years, each one bringing
    back a memory of a dramatic scene
from a musical, when voices bellowed and soared
    from faces unconfined,
and audiences filled indoor theatres by the thousands.

The light from the 24-hour news coverage flickered
    across the screen, mottling the room
with shadows that came and went.
    Death tolls and dire predictions repeated—
1 am, 2 am, 3 am, each one spurring him on,
    each mask he was making—a future buffer
between infected particles of air
    and a life that might sew hearts back together
or draft pivotal legislation
    or invent a new device
to ease the lives of millions
    or solve a mystery
plaguing the justice system for decades.

"When are you going to stop?" his family would ask
    as they saw the stacks of masks each week climb.
"More are needed now than ever," he would reply,
    scooping up the latest batch to deliver
to the churches and shelters
    where there was no shortage
of faces, of lungs,
    of exhalations, heavily-laden.

❖ *Tapas* (Self-Discipline)

The Tripled Tempo

The lavender dress the musician was wearing
   on the evening of her debut was not as precise
as the syncopated rhythm of her dazzling cymbals
   sending circles of light
into the tuxedoed and evening-gowned audience.
   It was not so much that it was a cheap fabric
but that the seamstress had been distracted,
   and her alterations were giving the shape
of the musician's body
   a strange pronunciation.

The tripled tempo of her symphony,
   however, made minds race
     and the audience had no time to think
about the disturbed stitching of her dress,
   their tedious pre-concert dinner conversations,
     the walrus-sized silence sitting in their cars
between cufflinks and pearls,
   the eloquent spin of Christmas card letters,
     the choke of dreams—
no time for any of this
in the bursts of copper flowers
   splitting the night into stars.

Later, once the applause had faded and the crowd had dispersed,
   she found herself with the liquid fire of whiskey by her side.
The desire to partake of this temporary ticket to oblivion
   crooned to her like the most seductive of love songs.
She picked up the bottle and held it, embracing it,
   gazing into the past.
From somewhere, the echoing of those days
   still reverberating deep within her sounded
like a faint pulsing crescendoing into a fire alarm
   shaking her back to her senses,
and she found herself walking,
   bottle in hand, out to the dumpster,
the sound of breaking glass even more beautiful
   than her dazzling performance on stage.

❖ *Śauca* (Purification)

Avalanche of Anxiety

The Wheel of Fortune contestant
   could not believe his luck when he was chosen
to be on the show. He had grown up on game shows—
   Let's Make a Deal, The Price Is Right, Family Feud—
and had been quite successful as a couch contestant,
   often hitting the buzzer of the cushion a half-second
before the TV contestants chimed in with their answers.

But now, with the bright lights and the pressure
   of millions of viewers, he was inside an avalanche of anxiety.
Preventing hyperventilating was his chief concern,
   more so than solving the puzzles. As he waited
through the other contestants' introductions, vowels
   and consonants swarmed his mind. Despite his calculations
of the probability of each of the twenty-six letters
   occurring in a puzzle, he felt himself suddenly inclined
to throw out the statistics and select dark horses
   like Q. He couldn't think straight with that giant wheel
just inches in front of him. The zeroes in the dollar amounts
   were making him dizzy. He definitely did not want
to faint on national TV. Slow, deep breaths
   he kept telling himself as Vanna moved toward
the first puzzle, the sequins on her dress blinking.

As the category was announced, his brain froze.
   He felt like he was in the middle of consecutive rounds
of sun salutations about to fall on his face
   after one too many *caturaṅgas*. He needed to find
his center. The wheel spun, the audience clapped,
   the blank letters turned into words. He was selecting letters
chosen by something beyond his left or right brain
   and winning and losing money faster than brokers
on a wild market day. The metaphor, even at warp speed,
   was not lost on him as he mentally fast-forwarded
through the gains and losses of his life,
     letting go of all that existed
beyond the very next breath.

             ❖ *Sūrya Namaskāra* (Sun Salutation)

The Unsolved Case

A hymnbook floated in the FBI agent's memory,
    its pages fluttering open in quiet moments of confusion
when a case had her stumped. Why this hymnbook appeared
    was a sidewalk without an easy ending. Her stomach was frail
with too many brownies, too much chocolate frosting,
    and too many late nights into mornings
ringing her eyes with unanswered questions.

How was she to buy bread, make coffee, and do laundry
    with a case unsolved? To her, the unsolved case
was a casino in a backpack: impossible.
    Debating whether or not she had the strength or patience
to carry such weight was impractical at this point.
    She had passed agent training and had been assigned to the field.
Curling up in the curves of question marks was not an option.
    With a gun on her hip and a badge in her pocket,
she moved forward to press the unsolved case
    into pieces large enough for the bureaucratic puzzle.

As she strode into another day relentless in its ambiguities
    and abundant with frustrations, she vowed to do no harm.
That was easier, of course, said than done.
    As vigilant as she was with her protocol at work,
receiving top commendations for her excellence,
    she was merciless in the internal chambers, persecuting herself
for the tiniest of things: the way she overcooked her omelets,
    the way her house plants wilted, her inability to speak aloud
what she felt inside. Gradually, she began to keep watch on her thoughts,
    patrolling the dark alleys of her mind, astonished at first by what she found.

Over time, as she resisted the urge to flee
    and remained as a witness
to the internal terrain,
    the space within her
seemed to soften and expand
    in a way she didn't understand
rebooting her system
    to where she was less likely

to slice the knife of criticism
    into herself
or into anyone else.

> ❖ *Ahiṃsā* (Non-violence)

Small Globes

The ophthalmologist felt as if he had rust on his knees,
   or maybe he was simply tiring of peering into the small globes
of eyes day after day. Sometimes, like now, his attention,
   galloped away and instead of thinking "iris" and "retina,"
he was thinking of the gleam of sun on railroad tracks.

The hazards of his shifting concentration taunted him
   like the songs of a jealous angel and reminded him
of when his diagnoses used to be precise as a single gunshot
   taking down a deer from hundreds of yards away.
If only some prophet could tell him what the future
   would be like, maybe he could float above the uncertainties
and let the riddles of each day dissolve with the grace
   of raindrops into soil, into rock, into streams that feed the sea.

Engulfed by too many future uncertainties to count, he centered into his breath,
   feeling the present flow of air coming in, air going out. In this moment,
he was okay. He began counting the length of his inhale
   and the length of his exhale, seeing if he could lengthen the out-breath.
Then, keeping his head steady, he took his gaze upward and paused,
   slowly returning to center, he then took his gaze down.

Looking straight ahead again, he then glided his gaze to the right,
   took a deep breath, returned to center, and then slowly gazed to the left.
He moved his gaze next diagonally, from upper right to lower left,
   and then slowly from lower left to upper right. Next, he guided his eyes
slowly from upper left to lower right, then lower right to upper left.

Gradually, he took a clockwise gaze
   followed by a slow counterclockwise rotation
before blinking rapidly seven times. Rubbing his palms,
   generating some heat, he gently cupped his hands over his eyes,
receiving the radiant warmth. As he slowly opened his eyes
   and moved his hands away,
rays of light began streaming in,
   bathing him with much-welcome glimmers of hope.

        ❖ *Netra-Śakti-Vikāsaka* (Yogic Eye Movements)

The Musical Mazes of His Voice

"No, breathe from the diaphragm," his choir director had admonished
    when he was in the sixth grade. If only she could see him now—
making his living by singing songs. "Our son, the vocalist," his parents
    would introduce him to their friends who would then, without fail,
ask him to sing a song, usually from two to three decades ago.
    Good thing his repertoire spanned the spectrum from musicals
to jazz to gospel to country to pop. More than anything, he loved
    to follow the colors and textures of a musical phrase
and to give it his own shape, adding some teal
    to the royal blue of C major, or a shock of fluorescent green
to a classical rhythm like the waltz or an *allegro con brio*.

Through the musical mazes of his voice, he travelled the world
    and traveled back in time. With no end of job offers in sight,
he sometimes felt he was the luckiest man in the world—
    to get to do what he loved—and then receive applause!
But sometimes in the periphery of his mind, a doubt
    would shake free: what if something happened to his voice?

He started gargling with warm water, salt, and turmeric at night
    and began scheduling several hours of silence a day with devotion.

For thirty minutes each day he curled the tip of his index finger
    to the tip of his thumb on both hands
        silently chanting the *bīja* sound *Ham*[1]
visualizing sixteen blue petals flowering inside his throat,
    the sacred gateway between mind and heart.

        ❖ *Viśuddha* (Throat Chakra)

---

[1] Pronounced "Hum"

The Emergency Switch

The ambulance driver had to remind himself to stop
   when encountering a red light
without the shell of the ambulance surrounding him,
   without the spin of sirens sailing him forward
past any constraints.

The emergency switch was easy to turn on,
   but not nearly so easy to shut off,
his entire nervous system staying on alert,
   lit up like holiday lights,
hours after his shift had ended.
   He couldn't help wondering if each patient he delivered
would recover, if a 1-minute faster transport
   would have made the difference
between paralysis and mobility, life and death.

He knew he had to let go of wishing
   he could reach into the cars
and turn down the volume of the stereos and iPods
   so that drivers would hear his siren
and give him clear passage. But he could not.

He felt his pulse speed up and his jaw tighten.
   He was going to end up in the back of an ambulance
if he didn't calm down. So he began paying attention
   to his breath, trying to keep it deep and slow.
He also started allowing himself time
   to loosen his muscles, stretching
into the tight spots gently.

What seemed to help the most,
   though he couldn't say why,
was to lie on his stomach, legs apart,
   with his forehead resting on his hands
stacked on top of each other, elbows wide,
   breathing comfortably in and out through his nose,
the drama and trauma slowly dissolving,
   a golden soothing warmth at his center resonating
with the heat pulsing deep within the earth's core.

❖ *Śavāsana* (Prone Corpse Pose)

The Peace of Mind Shop

If anyone had ever tried to tell him
   that he would be working full-time
as the owner of a consignment shop
   after graduating with a master's degree
in anthropology, he would have never believed it,
   intent as he was on studying a remote culture
on a distant island.

But sure enough, here he was, as the owner
   of a store specializing in the buying and selling
of thoughts.
         Invariably, the "I'm going to give you
a piece of my mind" speech preceded a lengthy reel
   of advice that was unwelcome, irrelevant,
or ungrounded.
   But what he had come to realize
was that these nuggets of wisdom were of immense value
    when delivered to the person who was seeking such advice.

It was a matchmaking business of sorts. People came in
    more than happy to dump onto the counter the piece of advice
someone had given to them.
        In exchange, they received coins, credit,
or a chance to receive the piece they needed.
   To this end, he was constantly cataloguing
and cross-referencing the topics of advice:
   in-laws, insensitive bosses, finding peace, vanquishing debt.

Here, he found his niche. On the city block
   teeming with consumers and their wallets,
word spread of this island, this oasis, this opportunity
   to trade in what did not fit for what did, and he could barely
keep up.

   When thoughts of a dissertation started zipping
through the back of his mind, he would lower gently to the floor,
   standing on his knees, leaning his torso forward,
feeling his heart opening as his hands reached back and found his heels.

Looking up, easing his neck back gently, he would then pause, reminding himself of the camels, how they are sustained
by what they carry deep inside, despite heat, despite drought, despite swirling sandstorms of doubt.

> ❖ *Uṣṭrāsana* (Camel Pose)

The Toy Maker

The toy maker was trying to remember the number
    of tentacles he had made last month
for the pastel-colored plastic jellyfish
    ordered by the gift store manager at the city aquarium.
It was useless. He couldn't even multiply the number
    of wooden goats he'd made by four
to see how many goat legs he had carved.
    His mind was just plain too swampy
with the thick waters of fatigue.

It was that toy cathedral he had built.
    How could he have known
how these tiny churches would explode his business?
    The fiery colors of their miniature stained-glass windows
snuggled up next to him when he tried to sleep
    and reminded him of the joyous dances his mind used to do
before he became "One of the Top Ten Toy Makers to Watch."
    He sat outside under the night sky for many hours,
the long sleeves of his despair drying in the slow light of dawn.

Then, within that ambrosia of twilight,
    the skies turned hibiscus-red and soft as rose petals.
Bringing his index fingers to his temples,
    he applied gentle pressure, softening into the moment,
into the new self he had unwittingly become, letting go
    of his piercing, penetrating internal gaze of self-criticism.

And in that letting go, something else began to flower:
    the sweetness of compassion
flowing with forgiveness through his veins.
    And as the fiery colors of his mind faded into peaceful pastels,
he slowly removed his fingers from the sides of his head
    with the relief of a child seeing a broken toy
miraculously brought back to life.

    ❖ *Śaṅkha Marma* (Acupressure Points at Temples)

In the Dissonance

The naked sound of E flat minor troubled the organist
    as it arched over the sanctuary for eight full counts.
The tone somehow had the color of beets
    and clashed horribly with the bright red carpet in the aisles.
He was allergic to this key, in addition to dairy products,
    and playing this particular offertory was like drinking an entire milkshake.
"If someone had a camera that could photograph my thoughts…"
    thought the organist as he played a passage heavy with chords,
"they might see me thinking about the tapestries of sound
    in an opera singer's voice
or the outdoor freedoms of working as a shipbuilder…"

He was lagging beneath the concrete blocks of his schedule
    and the snapped ends of his nerves were beginning to edge him
with the ripped rhythms of narcotics. Songs of the children's choir
    and their flowery faces were about the only places he could find peace.
He curled up inside their off-key voices
    and the beautiful music of sounds colored outside the lines.

Once that temporary respite faded away, he paused, unsure
    of how to exist in the dissonance spreading throughout his being.
Instinctively, he began curling his fingers into fists. He stayed like this,
    for quite some time. Then, taking the thumb of his right hand,
he pressed it into the point where the middle finger of his left hand had been;
    breathing into this touch, he felt the clashing of his mind and heart
begin to dissolve into a harmony, beyond sound,
    beyond thought, beyond anything he had known before.

    ❖ *Tala Hṛd Marma* (Acupressure Point on Palm)

Catapulted to Stardom

The CEO's success was soaring as she catapulted to stardom
   in boardrooms and business journals.
It seemed like everything she touched
   turned to gold. Profits were through the roof
and her schedule was teeming with new ventures.

After seven years of this momentum, though, she was beginning to feel
   trapped within a steel cage. Her husband didn't ask her to elaborate
on what she meant. Instead, he said, "What? Would you rather
   be screening for bombs at the airport?
Would you rather be dying from dysentery?
   Would you rather be a donkey trying to eat a jam sandwich?
Be glad with what you have for once, for heaven's sake!"

The pharmacy was already closed and he had run out of his meds.
   It was going to be a long night, she reckoned.
She had long since stopped looking
   for the glowing rays of solace in her husband,
so his outburst was not surprising. What was surprising
   was the image of a donkey eating a jam sandwich.
Where in the world had he come up with that one?
   Hungry, she opened the pantry and reached for the rice,
the only item present on the five wooden shelves.

As the rice cooked, she lowered her head
   to the marble kitchen table imported from France
and wept. Her tears knew something
   even her top advisors did not.
In that moment, something in her broke
   open as she boarded an unseen train
with all of her baggage,
   relinquishing, for once,
her pride and her need to know
   the destination.

      ❖ *Īśvara-Praṇidhāna* (Surrender)

The Competitive Blood

The coach was all about winning—
    not a day passed that he didn't pause
in front of his trophies, basking in their gleam.
    And when he sat out on the porch in his favorite chair,
eyes closed, he was often viewing replays
    of championship games in his mind. "Once an athlete,
always an athlete," his father had said long ago,
    and the coach felt the competitive blood
surging through him still.

He wanted the best players on his team,
    and he wanted nothing less than their best.
His practices began at 6:00 a.m. sharp,
    and if a player was even thirty seconds late,
he sent the whole team to do laps.

He lived and breathed the scores of the professional teams
    and had memorized the stats of the top players.
Yes, he supposed he was living his dreams of stardom
    vicariously. So when a player of his told him
he was going to sit out the season due to Covid concerns,
    he just about went up in smoke.
"You're going to let your fear of something
    you can't even see keep you from suiting up
and being there for your team?" he bellowed.

Now, weeks later, he had calmed down.
    He had even begun to understand why people
might prioritize their health and their family
    over playing a sport. As other players stepped down,
and as national league games were canceled,
    he stopped fuming, accepting (as best as he could)
the new normal.

He had even started, once a day, jumping his feet wide apart,
    bending his right knee with hips facing forward,
        extending his arms shoulder-height into a Warrior 2.
Bringing his right forearm to his right thigh,

sweeping his left arm across the front of his body and up, he gazed at the raised arm, the diagonal line from his back foot to his raised arm lifting a silent victory shout.

❖ *Utthita-Pārsvakoṇāsana* (Extended Side Angle Pose)

The Drive-Thru

The fast food worker smoothed the net that held back her hair.
    She loved working the drive-thru window—
not the one where customers were forever
    dropping their nickel or dime to the asphalt
or coming up a penny short
    but the one where she got to deliver with a big smile
a bag filled with just what the customer had ordered.

She was happy to provide extra napkins, ketchup,
    salt, pepper, mayonnaise, and mustard when customers asked.
But when she reached for the packets of salt and ketchup
    to take home for her family at the end of her shift,
she paused and retracted.

Even if it was free for the customers,
    she wasn't going to take company product.
Flipping burgers,
    pouring milkshakes, and cooking fries
was how she put food on the table for her kids,
    and she couldn't afford to lose her job.

When she got home and saw the bare places
    in her refrigerator and pantry,
        she took a deep breath and lit a candle.

At some point in her practice that evening,
    she sat with her legs in a wide V, feet flexed,
and reached her arms above her head.
    Taking her right hand to the inner edge of her right foot
and her left hand to the outer edge of her right foot,
    she turned to the left.
Looking up toward the vast twilight,
    she could feel the abundance of the life force within her
growing in the nourishment of her daily practice,
    the devotion of her breath.

        ❖ *Parivṛttopaviṣṭa-Koṇāsana* (Revolved Wide Angle Pose)

On Call

Incoming hit and run victim. Incoming from house fire, age eighty. Incoming
    heart attack. Incoming from construction site, laceration to liver.
There was no end to the emergencies
    and no end to the ways she could use her ten years of medical training
to put bones and organs and lives and families back together.
    So she was on-call,
even on the few days when she wasn't scheduled for a shift
    in the 24-hour ER in the heart—or bowels—of the city.
Drug overdoses, child abuse wounds—she saw it all:
    the after-effects of the cruelty, the insanity
of which humans were capable. She saw the miracles, too—
    how a one-millimeter difference
would have pierced the brain or heart or lung
    with the bullet or knife or the odd objects impaled from time to time.

If she had it her way, she would never clock out, never sleep,
    tapping into more time to continue stemming the tide
of the relentless need. But she had seen
    how just the slightest grogginess
could dim her focus just enough
    to miss a vital thread of the diagnosis
or to unsteady her surgical hand.
    So she took rest, like medicine, in proper doses,
conserving her energy, replenishing the life force of her vitality,
    taking time to walk outside and breathe fresh air,
to enjoy the natural light and quiet,
    far from the fluorescent lights,
blaring announcements,
    and beeping monitors
of her home
    away from home.

    ❖ *Brahmacarya* (Respectful Use of Vitality)

In This Wild Market

Hours before locking the door to his condo
   and starting the engine of his black sports car,
the realtor takes time to move through a *vinyāsa* flow,
   the sequence of postures invigorating him,
clearing his brain fog, preparing him
   for the long day ahead with a new client.

Visiting new listings, one after the other,
   and weaving through the traffic is a challenge he loves,
especially in this wild market, multiple offers
   flooding in, owners receiving more
than the asking price. He's never seen anything
   quite like it, people quitting their jobs, taking new jobs,
moving across the country, shifting from urban to rural—
   and vice versa. His client today says he's looking for
a two-story with a fireplace and a deck—and a room for yoga.
   In his thirteen years of showing homes, that's a new one for him.
Then again, meeting his clients masked is a new one for him, too.

Dedicating a space for daily practice—
   maybe he can do that in his condo, he muses,
remembering the day his five-year-old nephew
   had quietly joined him, copying his flow—
Downward Dog, Upward Dog, Warrior, Half-Moon.
   Later, he had shown his nephew Cat/Cow,
and oh, how they had laughed as they added
   a "meow" for the cat as they rounded their spines,
and a "moo" as for the cow as they arched their backs.

His client just may be onto something, he realizes,
   as he programs the address of the first listing into his GPS
so he can arrive to the first showing on time, calm, and focused,
   ready to flow smoothly from one location to the next.

      ❖ *Vinyāsa* (A Flow of Yoga Postures)

Shift and More Shifts

As much as he wanted to help,
   he was tired of picking up extra shifts
on top of his regular twelve-hour shifts.
   When he'd become a nurse twenty years ago
he went in with eyes wide open
   and he'd kept up with the pace
for a full decade amazingly well—but now,
   he was collapsing inwardly
in a way he hadn't known was possible,
   the PPE he now wore in the ICU
hiding his tears, the weary rings beneath his eyes.
   The calm, cheerful voice he sent out
didn't begin to match what he felt—
   a blend of fatigue and deep despair
weighing more heavily each day.

So when his wife asked him to join her
   for a yoga class on Zoom,
he said yes, mostly to keep the peace.
   He'd gone to classes with her before
and couldn't see why she loved them so much.
   Sitting with knees bent, soles and palms to the floor,
as they lifted the hips up,
   bringing their backs parallel to the ground,
     hearts facing the sky,
he wondered how in the world
   imitating a table could help anything,
marveling that people paid to do this.
   But if it made her happy, he could put up with it
and who knows, he thought, maybe one day
   something would shift—after all,
he reminded himself, he'd seen patients
   in a coma for weeks suddenly open their eyes.

    ❖ *Ardha Pūrvottānāsana* (Reverse Table/Four-Leg Posture)

Spanning the Gap

The professor of geometry had a pair of cats
    named Scalene and Isosceles
and a parakeet named Pythagoras who recited
    mathematical formulas from a wooden perch
inside a purple cage in the corner of the kitchen
    where the professor sat up past midnight
solving proofs.
        Quod erat Demonstratum—
writing Q.E.D. with a flourish after a particularly
    cantankerous proof made him feel as if he could fly.

Silly man, silly man, Pythagoras would repeat
    in these moments when the professor spun around
the room singing.
        Gradually he would slow to a stop
and stand with his legs apart, his legs forming with the floor
    an equilateral triangle, and with his arms outstretched
parallel to the ground, fingers extending,
    he would tilt, taking his right hand
down to his right leg, lifting his left arm up to the sky.

Holding this pose, breathing in and out slowly
    through his nose, he became the hypotenuse
spanning the gap between two extremes.

        ❖ *Trikoṇāsana* (Triangle Pose)

70 Hours Per Week

The lawyer who was known for his winning streak
   looked around his office at the books and file folders
from his cases stacked up in towers around him.
   He was due in the courtroom in less than an hour,
pressed yet again to finish drafting his opening statement
   in the nick of time. His stomach rumbled.
Though he could control the jurors with his rhetoric
   and hold an audience spellbound with his words,
he could not seem to begin to control his unruly bowels,
   a stubborn case of IBS plaguing him for two years now.
Whether his bowels would be stagnant or overactive
   from day to day was anyone's guess, and the uncertainty
kept him in a constant state of anxiety.
   He had tried acupuncture and going gluten-free;
he'd even tried various medications, but it seemed that the origin
   of the issue was hidden somewhere deep inside his mind.

Last week he'd actually had to excuse himself from the courtroom
   to make a beeline for the restroom. "Maybe you're working too hard,"
his intern had suggested, but 70 hours per week was par for the course.
   The firm had hired a new hot-shot grad last week
and he couldn't back down on his game now.

Standing at his oak desk, lowering his hips toward the ground,
   bending his knees, bending his elbows, pressing his palms to touch,
he rested a moment in a gentle squat,
   his fingertips aimed at the heavens
where a long line of lawyer-ancestors looked down from above.
   From the periphery of his subconscious, a voice spoke:
"Soon enough you'll be up there, too."
   He took a few deep breaths, stood,
wrote a couple more sentences,
   and walked as calmly as he could
      toward whatever verdict awaited.

        ❖ *Mālāsana* (Garland Pose/Squat)

Ocean of Intuition

How he could see the person who was about to call him
   before the phone rang he could not explain
any more than he could explain how he already knew
   what he or she would ask. It had been like this
since he was a boy when he'd had long talks
   at night with the visitors, his term for the people
who came from some other place to talk with him at night
   and whom he later saw framed in black-and-white photos
from long ago.

The psychic's challenge was not receiving
   the answers to what people asked him
but finding the right words to deliver the news
   from the beyond—and discerning how much of the future
to reveal. Even though someone was asking earnestly,
   was he or she really ready to hear if a loved one
was going to live or die, if a marriage was kaput,
   or if a debt was going to clear or increase?

In moments like these, he turned his attention
   to his third eye, center of non-duality,
ocean of intuition, letting go of logic:
   trusting the inner wisdom of awareness
to speak before he uttered another word.

       ❖ *Ājñā Cakra* (Third Eye Chakra)

Inside the Gaping Unknown

The narrow chance nearly eluded the furniture maker
    who was clumsy with intuition and even clumsier with timing.
He had always thought love would be abrupt
    in its arrival like a train whistle piercing the night.
Real as a football and just as unmistakable.
    He never imagined it might have the slow speed of a petal opening
or the nearly inaudible whisperings of willow leaves.
    So when the casual grapes of the moment turned unexpectedly to wine,
he climbed the rickety stairs of the tower of his confusion
    where he liked to wait out such periods of bewilderment.
Should he climb back down and ask what she had meant?
    Indecision, the straw breaking the camel's back.
He began thinking about camels and how they might be thankful
    to be rendered unable to carry the burdens of others
across scorching white sands.
    When he looked out the window of his tower of confusion, she was gone.

He had three options: 1) he could panic, 2) he could chase after her,
    or 3) he could pretend none of this had happened (or that he didn't care).
Usually he went with option three, but today it soured in him
    like an overly ripe mandarin. Was he just getting old,
or was it the repetition of this same story that was getting old, or both?

He sighed and looked at the framed photos of all his married siblings
    parading across his mantel. What if he never married?
Just voicing this aloud to his pet turtle Turquoise
    seemed to knock something loose
deep within the unexplored caverns of his mind.
    I could travel, he realized, seeing himself trekking up the Himalayas,
or relaxing beside a beach in Corfu, or translating a masterpiece
    at the Louvre onto a canvas on his own easel.
Maybe he would marry and maybe he would not—
    and for the first time, while sitting inside that gaping unknown,
he felt able to simply be there, instead of escaping, instead of racing away.

❖ *Santoṣa* (Acceptance, Contentment)

Lunar Luminosity

The day the seamstress went to the supermarket
    to buy staples was the day she began her asparagus diet.
It was something about their braided tips and the way they looked
    so sensible bound up in that particular green. Just the word asparagus
made her forget her varicose veins and the hamster her mind had become.
    It made her feel as if she could sit down at a sewing machine
and create her visions seamlessly, as if she could keep a bright pink hula hoop
    spinning around her waist, as if her lungs could have the strength of a moose
and she could belt out the Hallelujah Chorus in the middle of the produce aisle.
    As if she could travel beyond thimbles and straight pins
into the sweet green space of steaming stalks, and linger.

Back at home, she stepped onto her asparagus-colored yoga mat
    and placed her feet hip-width distance apart.
Reaching her arms out and up overhead, she hinged at the hips,
    folded forward halfway, and paused before lowering all the way
into a forward fold. Bending her knees and lowering her hips,
    she found a squatting pose, bringing palms to touch at the heart.

Then, placing her hands on either side of her right foot,
    she stepped back with her left foot, bringing the left knee
to the earth. In a low lunge, she lifted her arms up toward the moon.
    Her hands came back to the mat as she brought her right knee
side by side with her left. Lowering hips to heels, forehead to the earth,
    she found Child's Pose before gliding her hips forward onto the mat
and lifting her heart into Cobra Pose, then slowly exhaling back to Child.

Inhaling her arms up, she stood on her knees,
    then took a big step forward with her right foot,
bringing palms to the floor in a low lunge and lifting her arms.
    Bringing her hands back down to the mat,
she stepped the left foot forward, lowering her head, finding
    Forward Fold, her chest coming in toward her thighs,
the crown of the head facing the floor.
    Then, engaging the legs, she inhaled up halfway,
reaching her arms in front before lifting them skyward.
    Bringing hands to touch at the heart, she paused there

before beginning the second half of her moon salutation,
    feeling the calming, cooling sweetness
of the lunar luminosity glowing within.

> ❖ *Candra-Namaskāra* (Moon Salutation)

It Didn't Add Up

The accountant sat at the sunlit kitchen table
    in her new work-at-home office. Working remotely
had its perks, she thought, as her rabbit snuggled into the space
    between her feet. Sometimes she was relieved not to be interrupted
by co-workers popping into her office unannounced, and other times
    she was plain bored. The pandemic was still spreading, and yet the news
showed people gathering without masks or social distancing. It didn't add up.

Why would they take such chances? She liked for things to make sense
    right down to the last penny in the boxes and columns of her spreadsheets.
She would tabulate, calculate, and recalculate until everything balanced out.
    That's why her clients loved her—
so why couldn't she love herself? Why was her mind
    constantly digging holes in her self-esteem with sharp words of critique?
She felt the small feet of her rabbit on her leg
    and looked down at the quivering nose,
the loving eyes, the soft long ears.
    It was time to close up shop for the day,
time to close the laptop, and put away her files.

She went down the hall to her meditation room and sat on her yoga mat.
    Knees bent, soles on the ground, she reclined onto her back
and lifted her feet, drawing her knees into her chest.
    Extending her legs up, soles of her feet to the ceiling,
she paused there, like the corner of one of her ledger sheets,
    letting the reverse flow of circulation do its work.
Looking up toward the sky toward the planets,
    the big issues orbiting her mind suddenly became small.
Bending her knees and drawing them in toward her chest,
    she lowered them, bringing her feet to the floor.
Sensing the shift, her rabbit hopped up, curling up on her navel
    and closing its eyes, nestling into the warmth at her core.

        ❖ *Supta-Daṇḍāsana* (Reclined Staff Pose)

His Plan to Save the World

That the beggar was begging for smiles and square dances
  was not so strange. His lime-green flannel suit with plastic orange buttons
was what was catching the attention of sullen faces peering out
  of windshields at this unexpected addition to their xeroxed days.

The beggar had chosen the stretch of sidewalk between the local library
  and Catholic church. His plan to save the world had gone bankrupt
and now he stood eating a slice of canned pineapple
  in front of his sign: "Not a penny, a peso, a cinnamon drop,
or even a dollop of cottage cheese—just a big grin
  or a quick do-si-do please!" Mostly it was groggy mothers
with newborns in strollers who stopped to read the sign,
  and mostly it was the babies who smiled. Square dances?
None yet, but the anticipation of such a spirited donation
  fed him even as the hours spilled into days.

The truth was that he was lonely
  and no amount of fleeting smiles could lessen the lament
of loneliness pulsing in each and every one of his pores
  until someone—or many someones—could pause
to look into his eyes—his beautiful almond-colored eyes,
  his eyes of a hundred storms,
his eyes of untold grace, his eyes untrapped by time—
  But until then, there he was—not blinking, but not staring—
sitting open-eyed, a witness to all the questions without answers,
  the longings that could eat a person alive.

      ❖ *Satya* (Truth)

The Diamond of Lentils

A diamond of lentils on the counter.
   The chef shrugs his shoulders.
He knows he left them in an air-tight container
   the night before. There must not be enough ventilation in this place
is all he can figure. The lentil-diamond is one in a sequence
   of peculiarities that interlock in a chain stretching back to the day
he served the tomatoes before they had a chance to ripen
   and almost lost his job.

Science suggests such oddities are a way of coping with the stress.
   But then there is the curvature of the air when the images fly in.
He scoops the lentils into his hand and throws them away.
   The diamond lentil, however, will plow through his dreams.
It will upturn his quiet and leave unweedable concerns in its place.
   Light as dandelion seed, these thoughts unplant him.
His nerves seek the soil of predictability:
   that lentils will stay where he puts them,
that the air will remain solidly air, that he will know the difference
   between the mind of his hand and the hand of his mind.

Reaching his index finger to the indentation above his top lip
   where it neatly fits, he applies pressure,
the touch soothing his mind, slowing it down,
   giving him a calm beyond chamomile tea,
the gymnastics of his thoughts
   giving up their cartwheels and back flips,
his dizziness disappearing. Breathing into this touch,
   this stability, this serenity, he senses a slow return
of the self he could always rely on,
   the only one he trusted
with the recipe for his most ornate soufflé.

       ❖ *Oṣṭha Marma* (Acupressure Point Above the Top Lip)

Salutations to the Light

After four years as a car salesperson,
   nine times out of ten she could tell
from observing the face, voice, and body movements
    if a person walking into the lot
      was going to buy or not.

On days when her customers were highly agitated,
   pummeling her with hundreds of questions
and changing their minds frequently,
   she would look forward to doing a set
of Sun Salutations slowly to calm her *Vāta*
   once she got home, lingering for a moment
in Downward Dog, feeling her palms and soles
   in contact with the ground.

And on days, especially in the height of summer,
   when her customers were irritable, impatient,
and critical, and she, too, found her internal temperature
   heating up her *Pitta* with frustration bubbling to the top,
she would dream of Moon Salutations,
    the cooling calm of taking low lunges
      and enjoying the surrender of each Child's Pose,
        her forehead resting sweetly on the earth.

Sometimes, though, when the days were long
   and the few people coming in were painstakingly slow
in their movements and thoughts, she felt a *Kapha*-like heaviness,
   a sluggishness inside—and each hour felt like four.
On these days, she'd go home
    and take Sun Salutations with a quick tempo
   of dynamic movements, sweeping her arms up
in victory in each high lunge,
   energizing herself
    for the unpredictable
      days ahead.

❖ *Āyurveda* +Yoga

Witnessing a World

The reporter who covered international catastrophes
   from Tunisia to France to Russia
always kept a bag packed, never knowing
   when tensions would explode and he would be sent
to document yet another round of violence,
   tabulating casualties and pressing through protestors,
predicting the likelihood of the complete rupture
   of a regime, and trying to somehow translate
an entirely foreign reality into short sound bites
   to be aired on the evening news as people glanced
toward the TV in the midst of eating burgers and fries
   or salads dressed with vinegar and oil.

As he navigated through the cultures and crises
   as best as he could, the emotions he didn't have
time to process burrowed within his hips, knees,
   stomach, and neck. Years later when digestion
trouble rumbled and inflammation in his joints
   began to ache, he would, when lying on a massage table,
begin to weep, remembering with unsettling clarity
   the faces of those in the streets who had begged
him for help, calling him by name, their eyes
   arresting him with their despair, their faith,
their witnessing of a world coming apart at its seams.

For now, he did his best to stay focused,
   recoiling neither from the present
nor the future—or even his own past,
   aware of the power of his aversions
to control him, his tendency to bolt away
   from the mere thought of the possibility
of another incoming missile,
   the recently intruding thoughts
of his own fleeting life,
   the impermanence of every breath.

        ❖ *Dveṣa Kleśa* (Aversion Affliction)

With Compassion

Along the walls of his studio, the radio announcer had posted photos
    he'd torn out from all different magazines and newspapers
over the past thirteen years. He placed the faces there to remind him
    that his voice might find its way to the hospital bed
of a woman about to give birth for the first time,
    to the family of a teenager trapped in a coma,
to an athlete just out of surgery,
    or to an elder about to draw a last breath.

His voice might spiral out to a school cafeteria
    where cooks were preparing lunches for hundreds of children
wrinkling their noses at green beans or cottage cheese.
    His voice might travel into the squad cars of police patrolling their beat
or into a million other places…

He had, after all, no way of knowing
    in which ears
the syllables of his voice would land,
    and so, as he often did,
he brought his hands to his heart,
    one on top of the other,
feeling the devoted rhythm
    pulsing beneath,
remembering his listeners
    across the city, the country, the world,
with compassion,
    each with a similar rhythm inside of them,
each sharing
    the heart's emotional terrain,
the rich colors and textures of all the joys,
    all the sorrows,
everything in between.

                ❖ *Anāhata Cakra* (Heart Chakra)

Reverse Ransom

The burglar never calculated the probability
   of colliding with a pig in the middle of his escape.
It had to have been as probable as a stagecoach
   blocking the path of his getaway car.
Still, the way that pig intercepted his plans
   lurked in the back of his mind
like the curse of an unsent chain email
   as he stared at the pale walls of his hospital room.
His pride was scorched and his invincibility
   was being held in the reverse ransom of medical bills.
"Perhaps," suggested his wife who had been his bride
   at the for-better-or for-worse altar
twenty years before, "the aged pig had cataracts."
   The faces on the pennies in the pile of loose change
on the nightstand did not move.
   They pressed their laughter into silent gleams
and the burglar, his humor long spent, rolled his eyes and sighed.

Once he had recovered enough to be discharged,
   he was due to appear in court.
Would it be a hefty fine or jail time? Only God knew.
   How he had ended up here began with the comic book
he'd slipped beneath his jacket on his way out the door of a convenience store,
   nearly right beneath the manager's wearied eyes years ago,
that thrill giving way to another one—and another, the stakes always higher;
   unsatiated—his craving, his adrenaline, his need for something more.
But seeing a shadow now in his wife's eyes that he'd never seen before
   started churning something in his gut that would not relent.
"Everything you need is right here,"
   came a voice from some unvisited territory inside.
And he knew in that moment
   that although it would not stop the aching in his heart, or hers,
it was absolutely true.
   Drawing upon more courage
than it had ever taken to steal jewels or cash,
   he boldly decided, right then and there,
to return the loot from previous thefts that he still had hidden away
   as he stood tall and looked the necessity of rehab directly in the eye.

❖ *Asteya* (Non-stealing)

Hungry for Normalcy

Against the backdrop of sunrises and sunsets,
  the truck driver crisscrossed the highways
delivering necessities via the arteries of a nation
  hungry for normalcy. Delivering her loads on time
was something she prided herself on, especially during
  the thick snows and merciless ice storms of winter.

In her eighteen-wheeler, she felt secure,
  immune to the feeling of being adrift
that had plagued her youth and left her hitchhiking
  on the side of a dark freeway
more times than she could count.

The perils of the open road no longer frightened her
  with her big rig to call home, the cab of the truck
decorated with souvenirs from all fifty states,
  the 24-hour truck stops lighting her way,
thousands of miles spooling beneath
  the enormous treads of her tires.

And while she loved to pass the time
  with the banter of DJs on stations ranging from country
to reggae to Christian pop, and to catch up with friends
  and family on her cell, or to chime in on conversations
with other truckers on her CB radio, she made it a habit
  to take three full hours of quiet each day,
steeping in silence; it was her secret weapon
  in a world gone mad with chatter.

        ❖ *Mauna* (Silence)

The Acrobat

The acrobat could not remember a time
   when he was not turning upside-down—
somersaults turning into cartwheels
   into walkovers and handsprings.
Then there were all the days when he had run
   up and down the grassy strip in the side yard
determined to do an aerial.

"You're going to crack that head of yours wide open,"
   his mom had chided more times than he could count.
Sometimes he would stand on his head so long
   that, crying, she begged him to come down.
It was no surprise that a top-tier traveling troupe
   became his second home, the director
bringing him on board on his first audition.

That was three directors ago, and now the new director
   was implementing a daily mandatory meditation
for the entire staff, something about unifying
   their energy field as a team. While he sat there
for the required thirty minutes in absolute stillness
   and silence, his mind went wild, performing acrobatics
he'd never even dreamt of before. Yet as agitated as he was
   while sitting still, he entered a smooth, calm flow of focus
as soon as he was in motion.

❖ *Dhyāna* (Meditation)

A Living Temple

From her loft apartment overlooking the cityscape
   with its glittering lights and skyscrapers, she never felt alone.
The buildings befriended her in a way that language could not begin
   to convey. Their shapes spoke to her and gave her hope.
Even as people were tearing each other down, construction
   of new edifices and renovations of old buildings continued.
She loved nothing more than to sit at her drawing table,
   turn on her favorite tunes, and begin a new sketch,
breathing life into yet another unique design.

Across the room from her drawing table
   was a piece of purple carpet where she liked to practice.
Moving through sequences of movements,
   she entered her body as a living temple,
her *āsanas* as prayers. She wanted nothing more
   than to bring beauty to this world, one building at a time.

Daily she remained devoted to this offering
   of her time and talent, often forgoing parties and other outings,
delighting in making blueprints for a brand-new style
   of a homeless shelter to bring comfort to those roaming the streets,
the howls of their souls finding their way into her heart
   breaking open over and over like a blossom
that keeps flowering, rooted in a boundless flow
   of compassion and love.

      ❖ *Bhakti Yoga* (Yoga of Devotion)

The Virtual Realm

For as long as she could remember,
   the times she felt most content
were when she was in front of her computer,
   playing video games, posting to social media,
reading books on her tablet, and shopping online.
   To her, the virtual realm felt much safer
than any face-to-face interaction.

Her avatar was her saving grace, and emoticons
   were her friends. So it came as a surprise
to no one when she chose computer science
   as her major. Diving deep into the sea
of computer coding was sheer bliss: she loved to see
   what she could invent next and how one forward slash
or character of any kind could change everything.
   The power she felt as she sat at her keyboard
was intoxicating, and with world markets opening doors
   to different time zones throughout the day and night,
her sleep became meager and erratic.
   Deep down she knew something wasn't right,
but she kept going, unable to power down.

Sometimes, though, when she got a notification
   about a yoga class starting in an hour online,
she'd give in and take a break.
   Her shoulders and neck thanked her.
As she moved through the postures,
   she arrived at a standing one,
one she hadn't tried before:
   leaning forward, she balanced on one leg,
the other leg extending behind her parallel to the ground,
   her arms reaching forward and then out to the sides.
After so many long hours at the computer, she was suddenly able
   to be present in the 3-D world,
in the world of earth-water-fire-air-space—
   and fly.

       ❖ *Vīrabhadrāsana III* (Warrior 3 Pose)

The Frequent Flyer

The frequent flyer flew so frequently
   that he was never sure how to completely unpack
the coming and going of his thoughts
   zooming through the hidden spaces
where they had stowed themselves away.
   Hovering so often in the sky, feeling grounded
was no easy task. The cells of his body spun
   like compasses, clocks, trying to recalibrate.

Even when the businessman was sitting still on an aisle seat
   within the curved walls of an aircraft
or on the edge of yet another
   too-neatly-made hotel bed,
he was in transit, his mind moving ahead
   to a future destination. Most of the time
he did not even realize the flocking
   of his thoughts, the V they made traversing
the sky of his mind.

But little by little,
   awareness of the internal fluttering began
to present itself one realization at a time,
   building a nest within, a circular space
of stillness where he could rest,
   counting the length of his inhale,
the length of his exhale, eventually traveling
   further within than he could ever,
even on an international flight, fly.

          ❖ *Svādhyāya* (Self-Study)

A Continual Surrendering

The sun was setting, which meant the sun was rising
   for her family on the other side of the world. The red-orange rays
always gave her pause. This was her fifth tour of duty
   and, she hoped, her last. How she had avoided being struck
by an incoming missile or even by friendly fire
   while so many of her fellow soldiers had been medevac'd
stateside was something she often pondered.

How much longer, she wondered, could she survive on military rations
   and FaceTiming her children as they grew up
thousands of miles away?

At least she wasn't waiting weeks or months for mail
   as her father had when he had served. Looking up to the stars
each night, she remembered her strength,
   calling to mind the reasons she'd enlisted in the first place.

From the first day of boot camp, this experience had been
   a continual surrendering, relinquishing control,
loosening her ego's grip on wanting life to go a certain way.
   At the same time, she had become fiercer than ever
with a rock-steady center and a nearly unshakeable focus.

Over the decades, she had grown eyes in the back of her head.
   One footstep could bring her from deep sleep
to high alert. So when she woke in the night
   on a false alarm, she would kneel on the floor by her cot,
lowering her forehead to the earth, and reach her palms back
   to connect with her soles. Staying like this for at least ten breaths
allowed her parasympathetic system to triumph over her stress,
   and, recalibrated, she'd crawl back into bed,
     surrendering
       to sleep
         once more.

❖ *Bālāsana* (Child's Pose, variation)

Proud as a Peacock

The journalist smoothed the graying hairs of his mustache
    and glanced at the yellow and orange polka-dotted teapot.
It was one of the few splashes of color in the rental trailer.
    The thin mattress was as dingy as the sky
in this winter prairie town. He tried to imagine the empty fields
    lush with summer clover, and failed.
The fact that both of his wrists were free of watches
    didn't begin to explain why time was passing so slowly.
Why he had been the one sent out here to follow the murder trial
    was a question he asked himself each morning
as he ate at the town's only café. He saw men in Wranglers
    instead of pressed suits. He watched people eat links of sausage and fried eggs
instead of yogurt and bagels. He could smell the rich soil
    instead of perfume and cologne. Words to describe this world stuck
in his throat. He unsnapped the leather cover of his planner
    to check his calendar for the zillionth time.

He recognized the heaviness of the trial was weighing on him, stealing
    his appetite: there was a cloud cover in his soul, it was true—
though at least he was able to notice it, which was leaps and bounds
    beyond where he'd been even a year ago. Setting aside his planner,
he turned off his phone and got down on the floor on his knees.
    He brought his elbows together, palms to the ground,
fingertips facing his feet, pinky fingers side by side,
    and, bending his elbows, he leaned forward,
bringing the weight of his upper body to his elbows
    and resting his chest on his arms.
Extending his legs and, ever so carefully, lifting first his feet
    and then his knees off the ground, he hovered in the air,
proud as a peacock for every second he remained
    balancing in the thin air.

        ❖ *Mayūrāsana* (Peacock Pose)

Becoming Incandescent

When a soul began moving out to sea, he somehow just knew.
   He knew even before the round-the-clock nurses were called in.
After twenty-one years of working with hospice, he'd seen the full range
   of emotions, from a numbed shock to outrage to trembling fear
to confusion. Some even laughed, taking refuge in denial.
   His role was not to interfere but to simply be there,
easing logistics when he could, offering a listening ear,
   helping to explain the physiological process of exiting this life.

When the departing one was in pain or agitated,
   it was often more than the family could bear.
Sometimes, though, a peaceful glow emanated
   and the departing one became incandescent,
illuminating the unknown with exquisite grace.

He used to keep count of how many he'd seen leave,
   but after four hundred, he let that go.
Instead, each time another one crossed over,
   he would, after his shift, light a candle in his altar room,
sitting cross-legged, gazing at a cross hand-carved from cedar.
   Shifting his legs into lotus pose and pressing his palms
into the floor, his hands by his sides, he lifted his lower body
   up off the floor, transcending everything rooted to the earth.

❖ *Utthita-Padmāsana* (Lifted Lotus Pose)

Being a Student

"Your job right now is being a student," his father had said
   in no uncertain terms. This was when, at the height of the pandemic,
he'd suggested taking a job delivering groceries to bring in some cash.
   As he watched the number of cases rise,
he also saw his family's debts climb, and his anxiety level skyrocketed.

Which was he most afraid of: his parents dying from the virus,
   getting sick and dying himself, failing his new online classes,
getting evicted from his studio apartment,
   or not being able to get a job once he graduated?

He felt his muscles tighten, his whole body constricting,
   the speed of his thoughts moving faster and faster,
one worry breeding another. Some of his friends said
   their stress levels went down when they meditated
or did yoga—but the thought of trying something new
   stressed him out, the fear that he might not do it right
stopping him in his tracks,
   where he stayed, fretting,
his stomach churning.

   Checking the death toll again today,
checking his temperature again, reminding his family
   to wear their masks, the fear of death looming
exponentially larger than the fear
   of failing his upcoming final exams,
he stretched out on his back on his bed
   like a corpse, letting the rhythm
of his inhale and exhale soothe his soul
   at least for the time being
as he accepted his fear for what it was—
   a ferocious storm passing through.

      ❖ *Abhiniveśa Kleśa* (Fear of Death Affliction)

The Intricacy of This Life

Early in the morning, the microbiologist sat facing east.
   The rooster had not yet crowed. Her stomach was empty,
her coffee not yet brewed. She sat with spine elongated
   and breathed in deeply, filling her nostrils and lungs with fresh air.
Keeping her mouth closed, she then slowly exhaled,
   squeezing the air out. At the bottom of her exhale,
before taking a new breath, she drew the abdomen in and up,
   in and up, massaging the abdominal organs,
nourishing her digestive fire. This morning ritual,
   passed down to her by her grandpa, kept the ancestral line
of awareness shining at her core.

An hour commute into the city later, she would be suited up
   in the lab peering into the revealing lens of a microscope
to see what had grown on the agar in the Petri dishes overnight.
   The colors, shapes, and designs of the minute organisms
never failed to fascinate her and to remind her
   of the intricacy of this life,
the care taken in the exquisite configurations
   of even those things invisible to the naked eye,
unseen by the vast majority of the population,
   their heads down, their eyes searching
for the next incoming text,
   the next notification of something
that would either stoke or dampen
   the fire at their core.

      ❖ *Agni Sāra* (Excellence of Digestive Fire)

On Stage

While he waited for his number to be called
    for his driver's license to be renewed,
the actor took out his phone, scrolling through his photos
    of past performances at the local theatre.
He had been a police chief, a receptionist, a king, a drug addict,
    a calligrapher, a piano tuner, a photographer, a lifeguard—
and that was just in the past four years.

His closet was a collection of costumes,
    and his mind was a mix of half-remembered lines.
Comedy, tragedy—it was all the same to him:
    he loved being on stage, and no emotion, no scene
was beyond his reach.

"But you're so quiet," people who worked with him
    at the factory manufacturing measuring spoons
would say when they heard. What did that have to do
    with anything? he wanted to say, but kept quiet.

As he waited in the large waiting room watching people
    come in the door one by one, he tried to guess their occupation,
which scene had just played out in the ever-evolving script
    of their lives. The shoes were often a dead giveaway,
but with some people changing their shoes nearly as often
    as their mood, he couldn't always be sure.
Finally, he heard his number called
    and he stood up and began to walk to the counter,
as aware of his gait and audience as if he were on stage.

       ❖ *Līlā* (Divine Play/Drama of Life)

Third Month of Furlough

He was not going to lie: he was tired of having to ask people
   to step back from the paintings and displays. Couldn't they see
the signs? And he was even more tired of seeing the frustrated ways
   they looked at him as they sighed and begrudgingly stepped back
as if he himself had made the rule. "I'm not hurting anything,"
   some said in a surly voice, or "Give me a break."
Only once in a great while someone would turn with genuine surprise
   and apologetically say, "Oh, I'm so sorry, sir."

And thus, his days rolled by in temperature-controlled,
   high-security rooms where he stared at the same artwork and relics,
watching visitors walk in, pause, and move on.
   What was going on inside their minds as they gazed, he wondered,
often wishing he had a mini-MRI he could use to discreetly zap them
   and find out.

But now, sitting on his couch, watching four hours of re-runs,
   he actually missed his job, minus the madness. With a government job,
he'd thought he was safe, but now his third month of furlough
   was well underway with no end in sight. He couldn't sleep,
and his bowels were a wreck. "Sit on the ground, breathe slowly,
   and visualize a red color at the base of your spine,"
his niece who didn't eat meat or dairy
   or anything that tasted good, in his opinion, said knowingly.
It sounded like malarkey to him, but what did he have to lose, he thought
   as he hoisted himself up off the couch and moved earthward.

❖ *Mūlādhāra Cakra* (Root Chakra)

The Job Applicant

He was beginning to realize he actually missed going into an establishment,
   asking for an application, and then sitting there in an uncomfortable chair
with a clipboard on his lap neatly filling out each of the boxes.
   Now he sat at home scrolling through endless job postings
on his computer. Click, scroll, click.

He read the descriptions and qualifications, trying to picture the settings,
   and failed. When the job search engines delivered a new list of openings,
he would pause before clicking them open: Would this be the day
   when he found a perfect match? Would he be chosen for an interview,
he wondered as he uploaded his resume for the eighty-eighth time.
   And if so, would the salary even be enough for him to live on?
Would the work be something he could stomach? And would he stay there
   for twenty weeks—or twenty years?

The surreal nature of it all made his eyes blur.
   The bleariness of two hours of searching caught up with him
and his stomach was in knots. He couldn't eat a thing.
   He was either overqualified or underqualified, it seemed,
and he didn't know what to do.

"Remember who you are,"
   his wife who had passed away last year would say,
"any company would be lucky to have you."

As he heard her words echo inside,
   a soothing warmth spread through his core,
his solar plexus taking on a yellow hum,
   the rays of his confidence
slowly beginning to cut through the clouds of his despair,
   a glimmer of his former confidence starting to flicker,
coming back to life.

   ❖ *Maṇipūra Cakra* (Solar Plexus/City of Gems Chakra)

The Retiree

After forty years of clocking in and clocking out, he was through.
   He had photos from the retirement party to prove it.
No more performance reviews, no more staff meetings,
   no more wondering if a time-off request would be approved.
And no more knowing what he needed to do when he woke up.

The first years of his retirement had been nothing short of bewildering.
   It was like he was going through a whole system reset—in slow motion—
without any helpline or technical support to call.

Some of his friends had bought RVs when they retired,
   but why would he want to drive around in a makeshift house
when he'd spent his life paying off his mortgage?
   Others had started volunteering or had picked up part-time jobs,
and he wished them well, opting to stay in solitude himself.

Unshackled from the demands of the 9-5 world, finally
   he could do as he pleased. Without knowing exactly why,
he began sitting for long periods of time, with spine upright,
   watching his thoughts, feeling his breath flowing in and out.

After four decades on the job, there was no shortage of thoughts
   to watch. Slowly, though, as the years passed,
the reels of footage began to clear, and all he saw was color.
   Expanding into an undefined domain,
it sometimes felt as if he were floating. Hours passed like minutes.
   And, no longer bound by time, he finally felt free
in a way he never knew existed before.

        ❖ *Samādhi* (Liberation)

Night Shift

He had been working the night shift for seven years,
   the constellations and the phases of the moon watching over him
as he entered the prison, went through security, and began another round
   of keeping the inmates in check. Some of them had been in there
ever since his first day and he knew them by name.
   Of course much of the time they were asleep and anyway,
best not to become too friendly with the caged, his supervisor said
   at least once a day. When he wasn't walking the long corridors
checking the cells as he patrolled, his job was to sit at his post
   checking the video feeds of the security monitors, eyes peeled.

Once the inmates were deep in dreamland, though,
   sometimes he would pull up something interesting to read
on his phone for a few minutes. One day a hyperlink led him
   to Patañjali, and he'd spent months pondering the sutras.
Now he was slowly making his way through other sacred texts
   and inspirational readings on his days off.
"Anything good?" his co-worker would ask,
   when he saw him taking a short break,
and he'd nod, grateful for the ancient wisdom
   safely tucked inside his phone.

Soon it would be his turn to be on full alert,
   watching the security screens, and he sighed,
wondering which layer of his karma
   allowed him to be on the outside of the prison cells,
holding the keys, aware of yet-undiscovered illusions
   incarcerated within his own free-thinking mind.

     ❖ *Jñana Yoga* (Yoga of Knowledge/Self-Realization)

She Is Up

It's not even daybreak and she is up—
   already preparing ingredients for the day's meals,
chopping celery, making sandwiches, cooking soup.

Her children will soon need waking—
   and before long her husband will appear in the kitchen
hungry for breakfast.
   But first she needs to feed the dog.
Stepping outside to greet the morning sky,
   she notices a glimmering of sunrise at the edge of the horizon.

There's laundry piled up waiting for her
   and crumbs in the hall to be vacuumed.
Somewhere along the way,
   perhaps as the children are napping,
she'll be able to squeeze in a shower—
   the hours, the days tumbling one into another,
a need always reaching out
   to her compassionate embrace.

Later though, while her children play with their toys,
   she will stretch out for a few minutes on her back,
surrendering, letting her eyes close—
   remembering the impermanence:
how soon her children will sprout wings
   how soon one decade will become the next
how soon today will bloom into night
   and how soon the night will flower
into an exquisitely fleeting new dawn.

       ❖ *Śavāsana* (Corpse Pose)

In the Flow

His grandmother who trained him, initiating him
   into the laying on of hands, transmitting healing light
through the touch, must be looking on in amazement,
   thought the Reiki Master as appointments for distance reiki
began to fill his days.

Lately he was getting a lot of referrals
   for women with pelvic pain, ultrasound tests coming up blank.
When the energy moved in his hands as he worked from afar,
   he could sometimes feel blockages in the creative flow,
whether it was fear of conceiving (or not conceiving),
   a past miscarriage or abortion, or simply an inability to visualize
life other than the way it was or had always seemed to be.

In these cases, the energy was a burnt sienna
   rather than the hue of a ripe nectarine.
As the energy worked through, he could sometimes feel
   the rivers within his clients shift
from muddy, debris-filled tributaries
   to crystal clear and flowing.
And when they texted him afterward,
   sometimes their discomfort had disappeared,
sometimes the achings were gone,
   and their hands could rest
beneath the navel,
   at long last, with ease.

       ❖ *Svādhiṣṭhāna Cakra* (Second/Sacral Chakra)

Perhaps It Was the Shadow

The sacredness of his job was not lost on him
    as he stood beside yet another anesthetized patient,
his sterilized instruments in hand. At first, each operation
    he performed kept him on high-alert,
terrified by the endless array of all that could go wrong.
    But now, with hundreds of flawless procedures under his belt,
the challenge was to stay attentive and interested, and not space out
    on autopilot. To be able to remove tumors, transplant organs,
and stitch up the fabric of human skin was an accomplishment;
    he knew that, but knowing that did not stop the hemorrhage
of his regrets or fill the emptiness he felt when the stakes were not high.

It was like he was addicted to adrenaline. Or perhaps it was the shadow
    that still lingered from the few surgeries that had not gone as planned,
when despite all he did, the patient bled out right in front of him
    as the time of death was called. It was moments like these
that welled up in him unbidden when he moved into stillness and quiet.
    He sat, legs extended in front, pressing the sole of his left foot
into his right thigh and folded forward, holding his right foot.
    In the gentle hip opening, tears started to spill down
his chiseled cheekbones and perfectly shaved chin.
    Before, he would have swatted them away,
but today he just let them flow,
    not even bothering to wipe them away
before bringing his right foot
    to the inside of his left thigh
and bowing forward once again.

        ❖ *Jānu-Śīrṣāsana* (Head-to-Knee Pose)

The Dog Walker

It was a lot to keep up with—the home security system codes,
   the door keys, the schedules of which dogs to walk when—
not to mention the names of the dogs, their personalities,
   and each one's special needs.
Then, there was the weather to contend with:
   walking dogs in the rain or sleet
or beneath the searing sun was definitely not his idea
   of a good time.

Still, it paid well and he loved the four-footeds,
   so until he got a shot at an IT firm job, he would continue walking
the twin spaniels, Milly and Molasses, every day at 10 and 3,
   the Doberman and Chihuahua, George and Gemini, at 11 and 2,
and the skittish Labradoodle, Symphony, who surely had some form of PTSD,
   at 12 and 4. He took photos and videos for their owners to send in daily texts
just like a nanny would: after all, these dogs had more amenities
   than some children did.

At 9 each morning he sat on his meditation cushion
   taking several rounds of alternate nostril breath first.
At 5 p.m. each day he went to his mat and did a thirty-minute yoga practice.
   Lately, though, he was beginning to wonder if any of it did any good.
The doubts crept up like weeds along the path. He was tempted
   to roll up his mat and relax with Netflix instead. "I didn't know if the daily
walks really helped the dogs," he remembered one of his clients saying
   "until I stopped the walks for a month. No question!" With this in mind,
he dragged himself up to standing and took first Warrior 1, then Warrior 2,
   then Warrior 3, exhaling his boredom and frustrations, before bowing
in a standing forward fold, letting all of the doubts and distractions spill out
   of his head and dissolve into the resilient earth.

        ❖ *Śraddhā* (Faith)

The Ladder of the Spine

The tollbooth collector was paranoid
   about someone handing her a lizard
instead of a dollar bill. What allowed
   this fear to climb the ladder of her spine
and crawl into her mind? She didn't know.
   All she knew was that the surveillance cameras
provided little comfort in the middle of the night
   when gruff-looking men appeared at her booth.
At times like these, she pooled images
   of bright baubles and focused on clusters
of stars in the distance, thinking of how one day
   she would start a company specializing
in tasty treats for pets.

The fuel pump
   of her imagination was never closed,
and with every "Have a Nice Day" she offered
   to strangers passing through, she felt the wings
that grow from sitting inside of fear long enough.
   During the precious lulls when no headlights
or motors approached, she sat down, turning
   to sit sideways on the chair,
so that her hip and shoulder
   were perpendicular
to the back of her chair,
   turning again to rest her hands
on the chair's back.

She pressed her feet into the floor of the tollbooth
   as she turned. Her spine thanked her.
Hearing a truck rumbling
   in the distance, she came back to center
and eased her legs around to the other side
   of the chair, slowly repeating the twist.
And by the time the truck reached her booth,
   she was looking straight ahead,
smiling, ready to make change.

      ❖ *Parivṛtta-Sukhāsana* (Gentle Seated Twist—in Chair)

Searching the Crevices

The exterminator wondered if it would be ants, termites,
   or mice this week—or all three. How his income was birthed
from the death of hearts was something he pushed away
   from his consciousness with a powerful mix of denial,
distraction, and alcohol.
   Each day he drank the enthusiasm
and relief of his customers as though he were parched.
   He was saving the day! Delivering peace of mind!
Searching the crevices like a sleuth, he located
   the tiny hiding places and began to spray.
The chemicals would enter the small lungs
   of the rogue critters who had infiltrated the indoors.
His mission—to eliminate—complete.

So why did he feel so incomplete? He sighed
   and pushed himself through the rest of the day.
Once back at his bug-free home, no longer plagued
   by the swarms of work-related demands,
he began to stretch his tired body.
   Lying on his stomach,
with his arms by his side, he lifted his chest,
   extending his arms behind, like wings.
His legs, too, he lifted together as if they were one.
   He was becoming lighter and lighter…
as if he might lift off
   at any moment, no telling
where
   he might
land.

            ❖ *Śalabhāsana* (Locust Pose)

The Bliss of Being Utterly Carefree

The postal worker shifted the stack of mail
    from his right side to his left side,
making sure not to let any of the glossy catalogues slip out.

Daily, he traced his path from the day before,
    the week before, the season before,
unlocking the mailboxes for Apt. A, Apt. B, Apt. C
    before moving to the next apartment complex,
the next home, the next street, the next neighborhood.

Some people were waiting for him to arrive.
    Others left mail in their box so long
he struggled to find space to wedge in the new bills.

With more and more people switching to paying bills online
    and fewer people sending letters, he had less to carry
and more time to notice the curves of cursive handwriting
    and the angles of addresses handwritten in print
on the few brightly colored handwritten envelopes
    sprinkled here and there among the bills like wildflowers.

Though most faces he'd never seen, he felt, at times,
    he knew the Keisha, Sanjay, Alyssa, Estevan, David on his route
from seeing the catalogues and cards that came their way.

After a long day of hauling mail door to door
    in scorching heat or blinding rain,
he could not wait to take a shower and relax.

Refreshed, he would stand, roll up onto the ball mounds of his feet,
    heels lifted, and find his balance. Raising his hands
above his head, fingers wide, palms facing forward,
    tucking his tailbone slightly, drawing his navel in toward his spine,
he became a palm tree—his arms like two giant palm leaves
    glistening in the sun. In this moment, he was no longer an employee
at the end of a long shift. He was part of a coastal dreamscape,
    hearing the crash of waves upon the shore, smelling the salt air,
feeling the warm breeze infused with the voices of children laughing,

the squawking of gulls soaring through the bright blue sky, tasting, for a moment, the bliss of being utterly carefree.

❖ *Talāsana* (Palm Tree Pose)

On the Open Sea

He was never in one port more than a week
   and usually he was on shore less than two days at a time.
Being on the open sea was what he loved best,
   and being with people who were escaping
their daily realities and responsibilities for ten days
   was where he felt most at home.

The cruise themes changed month to month
   but what remained constant was the staff
being ready to make any customer's dream come true
   with sterling service and the scrumptious buffets
of gourmet foods served around the clock.
   Some people claimed they went on cruises
just for the food, and he believed them.

It used to be such a light-hearted job
   but ever since the virus had left entire crews
stranded out at sea for weeks
   with more travelers spiking fevers by the hour,
he had felt his stress level soar.

Now he wrestled with acid reflux, bloating, and indigestion
   of all kinds. The waiters brought him hot peppermint tea,
room service delivered ginger ale,
   and he tried sticking to bland foods,
but nothing seemed to help, tossed as they were
   on the high sea of change,
so when the ship quieted down at night,
   he would sit and watch the moonlight
shimmering on the water,
   and, curling his tongue, he'd inhale slowly, the cool air
tunneling in, then closing his mouth, he'd exhale
   through his nose, letting the warm air go.

In the quiet of contemplation
   as he digested the events of the day,
his stomach began to slowly settle
   as the night deepened,

the stars shining more brightly
   in the heavens, their light giving him hope
as he charted his course
   through the unknown waters ahead.

❖ *Śītalī* (Cooling Breath)

The Shared Fabric of Humanity

The early afternoon light streamed in
   through the sage green sheer curtains of her office.
The calm pale green glow seemed to soften
     whatever her clients said so that she could digest it
  and come up with something relevant—and hopefully helpful—
to say. Day by day, she absorbed the tragedies
   of her clients—from the minor slights by loved ones
     to full-fledged abuse. She watched their faces contorted
   with shame, embarrassment, outrage, and waves of sorrow.
She listened as their voices lagged and strained
   with the weight of bringing something to voice
for the very first time. Her office seemed to be some sort
    of confessional booth and crucible mixed into one
 as they kept coming back week after week.

In each client she saw a little bit of herself,
   who she had been or who she might have become,
each emotion, each reaction part of the shared fabric of humanity
   as she sewed up the tears in the fabric
with her words, reminding each client of their true nature.

She looked at the clock. It would be an hour
   until her next session. She exited her therapy chair
and came down to the earth. Sitting with a straight spine,
   she drew her soles to touch, her knees splaying apart.

Holding her feet with her hands, she opened them
   as if they were the covers of a book, reading the story
of her life, the lines on the soles commemorating the many miles
   she had traveled to reach this point.

Pressing her thumbs into points on the soles of her feet—
   a third of the way down between her second and third toes—
she breathed slowly, feeling the overactive energy of her mind
   begin to settle. And as she deepened her breath,
the inspirational quote that had been planted in her heart
   on the day she opened her practice
began, after many months of dormancy,

to resonate again,
the centers of her cells
   becoming luminous,
radiant, nourished,
   renewed.

> ❖ *Pāda Madhya Marma* (Acupressure Point on Sole of Foot)

Making an Ogre Smile

He was known as the one who could make an ogre smile.
   Having worked in banking, computers, and insurance,
he was used to dealing with frantic customers, irate customers,
   and customers who were utterly confused.
His magic method was to think of each customer
   as his most cherished mentor
who was having some type of temporary breakdown.
   This let him listen patiently and respond
from a deep well of compassion
   rather than flying off the handle
at the first inane or rude comment.

In the first minute of each call, he predicted
   how long it would take to resolve the situation.
Now that wait-times to get through to an agent
   had exponentially increased, people were either so weary
by the time the call began that they were eager to finish
   nearly before they began—or they were more fired up
than ever, their frustration incinerating any logic he offered.

Still, it was fascinating to see how one error or glitch
   could unravel even the most dignified person.
Using changes in his tone, word choice, and volume,
   along with variations in the lengths of his pauses,
he experimented to find the right combinations
   to remedy the situations,
always giving his best.

In the end, he worked to accept the fact
   that even with his expertise and best efforts,
some would praise him in the customer surveys
   and some would complain, or not respond at all.
Taking a bolster behind his back for support,
   he leaned back with his feet on the floor, knees bent,
opening his knees away from each other, allowing his soles
   to touch. Opening his arms wide and letting them rest
on the ground, he breathed in and out of his heart space,
   letting the torqued and taunting voices

of the day fade, finding contentment in focusing
   on the lifting and lowering of his chest
synchronizing with his breath.

     ❖ *Supta-Baddha-Koṇāsana* (Reclined Bound Angle Pose)

She Thought She'd Seen It All

Her days were full of starts and stops—
   and with a decade with the public transit system
under her belt—and a 10-year-service appreciation mug to prove it,
   she thought she'd seen it all:

the drunks, the drug addicts, the people in suits
   on their way to the interview that could change their lives,
the homeless carrying their belongings in plastic bags,
   college students cramming for exams, the faces
becoming familiar day by day, month by month,
   the hot blasts of air coming through each time
the doors opened in the summer months
   and the icy shocks of air when passengers boarded
in the winter keeping her mind from drifting onto autopilot—

then one day a passenger came on wearing a mask;
   she recognized the eyes, but what was with the mask?
She'd learned over the years not to ask.
   But now here she was, weeks later,
wearing a mask and gloves herself,
   wiping down the seats of her bus at the end of every shift
and even on her lunch break.
   And oh, how her heart sank
when she looked in her rearview mirror
   and saw passengers removing their masks
or lowering them beneath their nose.
   She wanted to stop the bus right then and there and get off,
counting the minutes until she could park the bus
   and retreat to the sanctity of her home.

After a long, hot bath, she would begin her practice.
   Her favorite part was reclining on her mat
and lifting her legs, flexing her feet, then lowering her legs
   like a lever to where she could hold them for five breaths.
She loved the feeling of energy that came to her core
   stoking the fire at her solar plexus,
helping her digest the difficulties of the day,
   preparing her stomach to receive dinner's upcoming delight.

      ❖ *Uttāna-Pādāsana* (Legs-Stretched-Out-and-Raised Pose)

Between a Rock and a Hard Place

The caregiver glanced at the clock—three more hours
   until his shift ended. In the past, when the time used to fly,
he had helped a man recovering from hip surgery,
   a woman who had had a stroke, an older gentleman mending
from open-heart surgery, a young lady who had been in a major accident.
   This time his patient had Alzheimer's and PTSD.
The slightest noise would agitate her and she often forgot
   who he was and why he was there.

As a result, the days careened between multiple realities.
   He did his best to stay centered, logging his hourly notes
as required by the agency. When his client asked him point blank
   how she was doing, if she was making any progress,
he was between a rock and a hard place: he wanted to be truthful
   and yet he wanted to be kind. Doing his best to find the balance
between the two, he comforted himself with the thought
   that perhaps she wouldn't recall each of his imperfect words.

But when her family members called
   to ask him the same questions,
he knew that what they wanted to hear
   didn't match the reality in front of him.
He hated to break their hearts,
   and yet he would not lie.
All of this took a toll
   and left him watching the clock.

Later, in the free space of his apartment,
   he would recline on the ground, bend his knees,
planting his feet into the ground and bending his elbows
   so that he could place his hands by his shoulders,
fingers pointing toward his toes.
   He would then press his palms to the ground,
lifting his hips, arching his back, coming to a full stretch
   of his arms, gently easing his head back,
and as his chest expanded and his heart opened,
   he felt the unedited truth

of his body, his day, his life
  begin to break free and sing.

> ❖ *Cakrāsana* (Wheel Pose)

The Pastry Chef

The pastry chef loved sprinkling sugar on the latticed tops of pies,
    knowing how the tiny sweet pieces would catch the light
as the pies sat cooling on the counter, the scent
    of strawberry-rhubarb filling the air. It was the little things,
the details, that made the chef hum as she worked,
    the designs in the decoration of the cake icing as delightful
as the cake itself. And the creation of new recipes—
    blueberry-pomegranate scones and chocolate-lavender muffins—
these were the moments when her spirit raised like cornbread batter
    puffing to a heavenly goldenbrown. Her life was not, however,
a completely sweet delight. There were the moments
    when things began to cave in on her, her balance collapsing
like a cake that fell with the slam of a door, the jolt
    sending a tremor through her very core. It was usually the orders
requiring zero creativity, like five-hundred yellow cupcakes
    with vanilla icing, that sent her into a stupor
where she questioned every ounce of her life, turning over
    each decision she had made like an ingredient
being weighed and examined. There was only so much
    cinnamon and brown sugar could do, after all, when the flour was stale.

She let the thoughts sift. And when even ginger's zest did not stir her
    from her stale state, she descended to the floor of the bakery office
lying face down on the chocolate-soufflé-scented carpet for a moment
    before pressing her hands into the ground by her shoulders,
her legs lengthening in a long line on the ground behind her,
    hugging her elbows in, lifting her chest, her face, her eyes
with the surrendering strength
    of one who knows what it is like to shed a skin
and continue on,
    leaving what is no longer needed behind.

        ❖ *Bhujaṅgāsana* (Cobra Pose)

The Page of This Day

The librarian's pulse quickened.
   Instead of a simple inquiry for a book
about eagles or cardinals, someone was asking for books
   about kayakers trespassing through private waters.

That was almost as good as the question
   a five-year-old had asked him as he passed through
the children's section: Why do dogs bark
   instead of talk and how do they laugh?

It was these golden moments splintering
   the roaring quiet of the library
that made him able to return each morning
   ready to shelve books about art and poultry,
ready to line up the spines, ready to issue library cards,
   ready to search the system for a line of legislation
that might stop the paddles of an intruding kayaker mid-stroke.

The thought itself was invigorating, as if he were suddenly
   able to hover diagonally on just his right hand
and the side of his right foot,
   like a dynamic bookmark, holding in place
this specific moment, the page of this day open
   and waiting, its words just about to be written.

           ❖ *Vasiṣṭhāsana* (Side Plank Pose)

The Woman with the Mismatched Earrings

The weary employee with the mismatched earrings
   did not realize that from one ear
dangled an amethyst crescent moon
   and from the other hung a jade square,
though a vague sense of imbalance
   kept percolating through her morning
to the point that she got up
   out of her office chair and stood
on one leg, pressing the sole of that foot
   into the grey carpet and the sole of the other
into the inner thigh of the leg rooting into the floor
   like a tree.

How long she stood like this,
   arms extending upward,
she could not say,
   though it was unmistakable how each breath
brought with it a sense of building calm,
   the stability and equanimity of an oak
swaying confidently
   even in the most turbulent of gales.

❖ *Vṛkṣāsana* (Tree Pose)

On Another Planet

He switched off his phone on Tuesdays at 5:45 p.m.
   right before he walked into yoga class.
The first time he'd gone to class, he'd walked into the classroom
   right at 6, shoes on, notification chimes on his phone
choosing that precise moment to sound. No one said a word.
   As he found a mat and sat down, shoes still on,
he had the distinct feeling he had landed on another planet.

He had to admit he was still surprised he'd ever gone to class
   in the first place—or returned for a second class.
That was five years ago—all of it starting with a flyer
   one of his tenants had given him for a free class.
He worked out at the gym five times a week
   so strength was no issue, but some of those stretches
really blew him away. First it was the sheer challenge
   of trying to do a forward fold or arch his back
that kept him returning week after week. Then he started
   trying out some of the poses during commercial breaks
when watching football and basketball games.

"You seem different," his sister said when she flew in to visit.
   It was true. Somewhere along the way, he found himself
actually forking out the cash for a long overdue new roof
   on his properties rather than doing a patch job
for the umpteenth time. It was as if he was actually starting
   to care, rather than just checking off
receipt of the rent checks on his to-do list each month.
   He'd started preparing some of his meals at home, too.
He hadn't planned to stop eating fast food; he just found
   that his car was no longer magnetized to the drive-thru
on a nightly basis anymore. "You actually listen now,"
   his sister was saying, and he realized she was right
as he turned his full attention to her the way he'd learned
   to notice over the years the nuances of his breath.
And though he was, for some reason,
   nearly always on the verge of quitting yoga,
somehow, like now, just enough determination to continue
   found him, right when he needed it most.

❖ *Sādhana* (Spiritual Practice)

A Dream Job

She used to love nothing more than the challenge of a new route
   and the responsibility of carrying hundreds of people
through the skies safely, her eyes keen to the output of critical data
   appearing on the dials on the cockpit control panel.
A windstorm, hailstorm, or any other kind of weather event
   never fazed her; in fact, she welcomed the added challenge.

Thanks to the airfare discount benefits for airline employees,
   she and her family had crisscrossed the world.
Truly, it was a dream job, the salary more than enough.
   But lately she found herself wondering how much it all mattered.
Was she not just flying planes here and there and back again?
   Why was she noticing how so few passengers ever paused
at the cockpit as they deplaned and even fewer ever said "thank you"?
   Had it always been this way—or was she just more sensitive
now that the thrill of mastering her job was wearing off?

She didn't dare mention any of this to her co-pilots,
   and certainly not to management or her family,
but each day grew heavier than the one before.
   On one particularly cloudy day, she recalled a visit overseas
when she had attended a kirtan, and how joyous she had felt
   without understanding any of the words.
On a break, she looked up "kirtan" on her phone
   and soon the sounds of Sanskrit were soothing her soul.
Every time she felt like resigning, she listened, the melodic phrases
   somehow restitching what was unraveling within, the Sanskrit syllables
resonating in such a therapeutic way that she found herself
   no longer dreading her next flight
but instead looking forward to the next journey
   of unfamiliar rhythms and melodies, their intrinsic nectar reviving her,
renewing, sound by sound, the symphony of her soul.

       ❖ *Mantra* (The Yoga of Sound)

The Butcher Who Lost His Flow

The butcher who lost his flow
   amidst the seemingly endless hours
of carving, slicing, packaging, and weighing
   stared at his cutting board,
which stared back at him.
   This went on for quite some time,
silence ricocheting
   at odd angles
as he began looking into the silver gleam
   of the blade of his largest knife
as if it held the answer
   to the question he didn't know how to ask,
as if it held the portal
   through which his smooth rhythm had fled.

Receiving no reply, he sighed,
   reclining on a silvery-grey mat
on the linoleum,
   still wearing his white smock.

Placing his hands beneath his sit bones,
   palms facing down, he hugged his arms in close
and pressed into his elbows, arching his back
   into the arc of a leaping fish,
letting the top of his head
   rest gently on the mat,
an ocean of air swimming in waves
   beneath the bridge he had made of himself,
     spanning the distance
   from meticulous methodology
to spontaneity
   and all of the measured and unmeasured
meters contained therein.

            ❖ *Matsyāsana* (Fish Pose)

The Tantrum of Her Mind

As she styled her hair and chose her clothes for the day,
   she wondered: will I be yanked into a press conference today?
As a public official, any time a major news story broke,
   the media was on the line, asking her to give a public statement.
She had gotten used to the microphones and bright lights
   and reporters lobbing the most unexpected questions her way,
but her body was starting to rebel. Sometimes it was insomnia
   or acid reflux; lately, it was migraines.

She was trying a mix of allopathic and alternative approaches,
   but it was still very much a work-in-progress. "Restorative yoga
is what helped me with mine," a colleague had texted her last week,
   and while she tended to recoil from anything sounding the least bit New Age,
she was at her breaking point. It was too hard to attend any public classes
   due to people invariably cornering her before or after class, eager
to have some one-on-one time to deliver their request for legislation.

But now that Zoom had removed the need to go to a studio,
   she was willing to give it a try. She logged in, keeping her video feed off,
keeping her microphone muted, and began gathering the props—
   a blanket, a yoga block (or book), a bolster (or pillow), and a folding chair.
"You'll just basically lie on the ground in different positions," her friend
   had said, and she couldn't imagine how that could possibly help.

As the minutes ticked by in the first pose, she was sure
   she was wasting her money—and her time, but as the class went on,
the tantrum of her mind began to ease, and when the class came to a close
   with a resounding "Om," she already knew
she'd be logging in for another class again sometime soon.

        ❖ Restorative Yoga

The Aloe Vera Shop Employee

The man who worked at the aloe vera shop
   was not unaccustomed to the skepticism
of first-time customers.
   "So the goop inside
this plant can really help me?"
   their raised eyebrows would ask. He would nod,
reach behind the desk, and pull out
   several small vials pulsing imperceptibly
with the gelatinous prayer composed
   of ancient syllables of biological design.

These free samples were tucked into purses
   and pockets of those who did not yet believe,
who had not yet been blessed
   by the jagged plant's humble offerings.
Asking for nothing but rocky soil,
   sunlight, and occasional water, it regenerated
generously. He remembered this when expenses
   for the store overshadowed its profits,
which was most of the time.

A shrine for hope,
   the store remained open, even on slow days
when fewer than twenty people stopped by.
   He concentrated on the designs of the green leaves,
sometimes for hours at a time,
   as if they were a *yantra*.
And in the silence of the empty hours, he could feel
   himself becoming increasingly rooted
in his convictions, able to withstand long periods
   of drought, confident of what was beneath
his skin, so that when pressed, he flowed,
   when broken open, he resealed, a quiet green
humming through him all the while.

            ❖ *Dhāraṇā* (Concentration)

The Warehouse Manager

The warehouse manager enjoyed being largely exempt
    from the outside world and its trappings of coat-and-tie expectations.
Inside his warehouse, in his jeans, T-shirt, and boots, he was king.
    Each morning, cup of coffee in hand,
he'd stroll through the aisles, checking on shipments
    and the stock unloaded in the night. The night crew, well aware
of the morning inspections, made sure not to miss a beat.

The manager was equally fastidious and easy-going. It was an odd mix,
    but as long as every corner of every box was where it needed to be,
the tyrant was a lamb. He would chat, joke, even whistle,
    as long as all was well. But when he became silent with a brooding glare,
look out! Once it was rats, another time a mouse,
    twice insects multiplying rapidly and perforating the product seals,
three times incorrect tallies, and once—pilfered stock.
    He thought he'd seen it all—until now—this new invisible threat
was driving him mad, keeping him up at night. Even with the PPE
    and temperature checks, how could he be sure?
What about the asymptomatic carriers? He vacillated erratically
    between keeping the news on 24/7 and shutting it off completely.
Orders were up, which meant his stress level was up,
    and even though profits were increasing, more than once
he'd been tempted to walk out and never come back.
    His next-door neighbor, indefinitely furloughed,
was making almost as much as he was—or was it more?

Every day, packages arrived on the neighbor's doorstep
    as they never had before, his purchases bolstered
by hefty unemployment federal aid. He sighed.
    In his head, he heard the words of his grandpa long departed,
"If something's worth doing, it's worth doing right!"
    He set down his clipboard and pen, took off his baseball cap,
and reached his arms out wide, lifting them until they were overhead,
    and then, hinging at his hips, exhaling, he folded forward,
bringing his head toward the ground. Inhaling, he reached his arms
    in front as he rose to standing, arms to the sky,
before exhaling his arms back down by his sides.

He continued ten more times like this
before returning his cap to the top of his head,
   picking up his clipboard,
and, with fresh ink and renewed focus,
   began a brand-new tally.

❖ *Uttānāsana Vinyāsa* (Forward Fold Flow)

In the Stillness

The cultivator of silence
   started withdrawing his senses
on the day he learned that life as he had known it
   was an illusion, the scaffolding falling away,
leaving him without anywhere to stand,
   except in the middle of the nothingness
beneath which everything was raw
   with never-before-felt colors:
from sour reds to bitter blues
   to a purely peaceful colorless balm beyond.

Making of his silence a rich cave of quiet,
   he feasted upon the absence of sound.
In the stillness, he travelled through
   the many corridors of his mind, even losing himself
sometimes in their mazes, returning each time
   with a new way to live within his own skin,
letting the weathers move through him,
   even the tornadoes threatening to tear apart
the very building of his bones.

And along the way,
   the Siren-songs that used to lure him
began falling away, the sea-depths of his consciousness
   pulling him in, its tide stronger than anticipated,
the tethering of shore slipping away.

Seagulls passing overhead had seen this all before—
   the freefloat of a soul with no lifeguard in sight,
riptide churning at the jetty
   pointing like a finger towards the immeasurable,
the silence of the never-seen-before sand
   at the bottom of the sea
beginning, for the first time, to be heard.

      ❖ *Pratyāhāra* (Withdrawing the Senses)

The Sirens of Fear

The emergency dispatcher was tired—
   tired of working the night shift,
 tired of the constant flooding of frantic voices
   into her ears, her mind, her heart—
the impossibility of ignoring the violent acts
   taking place behind closed doors
as victims struggled for breath—
   the pressure of knowing each second—
each half-second—mattered immensely
   and could easily determine
whether a person lived or died.
   Even though the lights in the office were bright,
there was a heaviness, a darkness in the night shift,
   and it weighed down her lungs
like an elephant stepping on her chest.
   She kept the radio on, she drank coffee,
her nervous system on high alert
   for the next incoming call.

Of course the times when the right words came
   at just the right moment and she became a vital part
of the rescue made the long hours and stress worth it.
   She imagined the children, the parents, the friends
of the revived one rejoicing. But still it was terrifying
   when she heard the gasping, the screams, the descriptions
of gunshots, hemorrhaging, seizures, strokes—

So when the sirens of fear inside her started wailing,
   she raised her right hand, her palm facing forward,
and took four slow, deep breaths—
   inviting peace in with the inhale,
and surrendering her fear on the exhale,
   her focus sharpening like a scalpel,
her body relaxing,
   her mind slowly becoming
noticeably less crowded.

      ❖ *Abhaya Mudrā* (Hand Position of Fearlessness)

With the Economy Like It Was

The smiling daughters, sons, and spouses
   in the framed photos on the desks watched him
as he consolidated garbage from individual trash cans
   into large garbage bags to take out to the dumpster.

Inside his vest with the company name stitched on the back
   a stampede of hoofbeats thundered each time he emptied the bags
into the dumpster. The thought of something that had been thrown away
   by mistake being sent, by his hands, to the dump troubled him greatly.
As his nightmares captured each smash and crumble of the trash compacter,
   he became so irritable that his nerves lit up like the coils on a stove.
He longed for a vacation at a resort—or even a job at a resort—
   where he could feast upon roast beef and shrimp
instead of bologna and Spam.
   But for now, with the economy like it was, he was stuck.

Each morning before he left for work, he'd gotten into the habit
   of bending over to try to touch his toes. He never quite made it,
those last inches eluding him every time. Instead, he wrapped his arms
   around the backs of his legs with his head dropped, knees bent.
This at least got the blood flowing
   and seemed to calm him down somehow.

Then, after standing back up, he would spread apart his feet
   and face them to the left. Lifting his arms to shoulder level,
T-position, parallel to the floor, he bent his left knee and lowered his hips—
   connecting with his warrior self.
Slowly bringing his right forearm behind his low back
   and scooping his left arm in an arc overhead,
he gazed upward, strengthening the contact between his feet and the floor,
   the muscles in his thighs reminding him of his strength
and of all the toxic thoughts he could toss away,
   one deep breath at a time.

      ❖ *Viparīta Vīrabhadrāsana* (Reverse Warrior)

The Green Song of Faith

After clearing the fields, tilling the soil, watering the crops,
    harvesting them, and taking them to weekly markets to sell,
the farmer felt each of his years each time he took a step forward.

With the volatility of the weather mixing with the volatility of his crew,
    he didn't know how much more he could take.
It used to be that simply seeing the new green leaves
    unfurl into a blanket of green across the fields
was more than enough to counteract any stress or strain—
    the green song of faith drowning out everything else.

But after eighteen years, it had all become routine,
    and his boredom and despair began to eat through his peace
like the bugs that sometimes invited themselves to feast in his fields.
    The farm had been in his family for generations
and he hated to let it go—besides, what would he do instead?

For as long as he could remember, he'd been rising at dawn
    and working until sundown, every wrinkle in his face
testifying to this truth. Thankfully, some people out there
    were devoted to fresh organic produce —
or else he'd be out of a job.

He went out to the barn and sat in the chair
    made by his uncle long ago, and with spine long,
he placed his palms, facing up, on his lap,
    joining the tips of his ring fingers to the tips of his thumbs,
and stayed there for fifteen minutes, smelling the coming rain,
    hearing the wind picking up, tasting the sweat from his brow,
feeling the earth beneath his feet recharging his battery,
    bringing vigor and vitality, rebuilding his confidence,
emptying his mind of everything—until his wife rang the bell
    calling him in to a home-cooked meal
of his own harvest seasoned with basil and cilantro
    from their own herb garden out back.

    ❖ *Pṛthivī Mudrā* (Hand Position, Earth Element)

The Dragon Maker

The dragon maker sat on a bench at the bus stop
   with the unsewn head of a dragon in her hands,
the red felt of its unstuffed face
   gaping half-stitched as cabs, trucks, and motorcycles
roared past, the birth of this dragon unnoticed.

And so it was that she brought creatures to life
   during the transit time between her jobs,
her bag of supplies strapped inconspicuously to her shoulders,
   her fingers pulling the thread in and out
of ears, necks, torsos, limbs, claws, and tails
   as weathers and days passed by the smudged windows of the bus.

It was only once she made it home
   and had fed and bathed the children, washed the dishes,
watered the flowers, and paid the bills
   that she could fill the felt forms
not just with cotton stuffing
   but also with prayers she offered
to shape the heart of the being that would one day
   be held in the arms of a child, softening
long hours of night, muting the stab of voices arguing,
   inviting daydreams of far-off places.

Tired from her day
   and thinking of letting her most recent dragon
go out into the world,
   she sat quietly, then reclined her upper body onto the ground,
her knees bent, soles of the feet on the floor. She gazed up
   through the ceiling on up to the sky.
Lifting her feet so that her soles faced the moon,
   with her knees still bent,
she held her feet in her hands, becoming,
   for a moment, a happy baby,
rocking slowly back and forth, soothing her system,
   calming her mind, taming the dragon
that still sometimes called her heart home.

❖ *Ānanda Bālāsana* (Happy Baby Pose)

Polynomials Popping into Her Mind

As the engineer reapplied her eyeshadow,
   she thought about the sine and cosine of the curves
she was making with shimmery gray.
   Polynomials popped into her mind
at the most inopportune times—
   while making jambalaya, purchasing silk pajamas,
playing Bingo with her kids.
   The silver wheels of her mind
never stopped spinning: What was the mathematical formula
   for the sound of a wheeze or the smell of sewage?
If there were calculations for these, she thought,
   then maybe they could be eliminated.
When she tried to bring herself into focus, round and full like a zero,
   she found her mind bound into a figure eight,
or worse yet, into the knots of a two or six.
   Seeking refuge, she reclined on the parallel lines of the equal sign,
even when the equation remained unresolved.

For now, she sat on the plush carpet of her home office
   with her knees bent, hands and feet on the ground,
fingers pointed toward her feet. Pressing into her palms and soles,
   she lifted her hips up until her back was parallel to the ground
and visualized the rectangle her body was making with the floor,
   calves and arms parallel, right angles forming
at her knees and shoulders. She then sat back down,
   spine upright, legs extended in front of her,
palms still touching the ground. Lifting her hips
   and pointing her toes toward the carpet,
she realized she'd made a 45-degree angle
   of her legs with the earth, becoming for a full minute
a right triangle, forgetting for this moment
   anything other than the strength
of her arms and legs supporting her,
   the beautifully balanced flow of her breath.

       ❖ *Pūrvottānāsana* (Upward Plank Pose)

In These Quiet Hours

She hated getting up at 4 a.m.
   even though the quiet at this hour
was as sweet as ripe melon.
   The electric lantern in front of the drycleaning store
flickered. Enthusiasm was difficult in this night part
   of the morning. The tremor of excitement
in the store owner's heart when she arrived in America
   had quieted. Her days here in the nation's capital—metallic.
The people's voices were bells, wanting, wanting.
   She had thought America would be baseball and Hollywood,
hamburgers and success. She missed the way
   matches in her mother's sure hands
lit the wood stove in her faraway home.
   All the lessons, all the facts crammed into her head,
all the money saved, and now, a successful American
   sending money back home—
the only place her heart sang without prompting.

In these quiet hours before the world started
   zipping and zapping with its full force of calls, texts,
and traffic, she lit a candle and remembered
   her mother, her homeland, and all that was dear.
Today, she also lit some incense softening the air
   with its gentle scent and found herself lowering into a lunge
with her left foot forward, bowing in obeisance.
   Lowering her hands to the ground,
she straightened her left leg to standing,
   lifting her right leg behind, parallel to the ground.
Keeping her right hand on the ground, she swiveled her torso
   to the left, lifting her left arm skyward.
In this position, she soared, traveling all the miles
   that separated her from her motherland,
eclipsing the distance a bit more with each elongating breath.

      ❖ *Parivṛttārdha Candrāsana* (Revolved Half-Moon Pose)

On the Cusp

The artist threw his hysteria from the bridge
   in an effort to subsidize his sanity.
It was a myth, he insisted, that artistic focus skewed reason.
   What was reason anyway, he wondered, but a sundial
reading the light differently at different times.
   It was no use to try vacuuming out
all the artist stereotypes from the creases of generations.
   He touched the buckle at his waist.
It was the same buckle that had belted his grandfather's pants
   as he plowed row after row of corn, as he examined the shades of color—
white, cream, yellow, gold—as he arranged the ears on tables
   at the farmer's market. "You are two sides of the same coin,"
his mother would say, her voice bent between pride and dismay.
   It was not unlike the shape of her tone when she realized
a repeating pattern in a design she could not define.

In moments like these when he's on the cusp
   of fragmenting into uncountable pieces,
he remembers what someone once told him
   about transmuting his sorrow and struggle into art.
Forming his body into a paintbrush or a calligraphic pen,
   he pauses in a plank—his palms pressed firmly into the ground,
arms supporting him, his body elongated, legs extended, feet flexed,
   toes curled under. Thinking of all the obstacles, all the struggles,
he bends his elbows, exhaling, feeling his full strength, lowering his body
   until his upper arms are nearly parallel
to the paint-splattered drop cloth protecting the ground.
   He's never felt so invincible.
In the face of all past, present, and future rejections,
   he holds firm, he holds steady—and breathes.

     ❖ *Caturaṅga-Daṇḍāsana* (Low Plank Pose)

Opening to the Heavens

The astrologer looked up one night at the constellations,
   noting Venus' distinctive glow. Now that her business was booming,
she was no longer sleeping well, flummoxed by a never-ending stream
   of requests for appointments, requests for personalized predictions,
the requests multiplying as quickly as the virus was replicating.

Somewhere along the line, the queries had shifted: now instead of asking
   when the pandemic would end, clients were asking her to predict
when the next variant would arrive. In their eyes she saw their tears
   as they beamed in from all parts of the world, appearing on the screen
in her living room, asking if their friends with Covid would survive.

Sometimes it became too much for her to bear. In moments like these,
   she wanted to shake loose the planets from their orbits and scatter the stars.
Adjusting the large amethyst crystal she kept by her computer,
   she went to her bedroom and turned off the lights.
Lying on the iridescent carpet, she looked up
   at the glow-in-the-dark stars illuminating her ceiling.

Bending her knees and placing her feet on the ground hip-width distance apart,
   her arms resting by her sides, she lifted her hips slowly, arching her back,
tucking her chin slightly, her heart opening to the heavens,
   the arc of her body bridging the known and the unknown
with each gentle wave of the intuitive flow of her breath.

        ❖ *Setu-Bandhāsana* (Bridge Pose)

Miles Logged and Fares Accrued

The cab driver wondered who would flag him down next
   and where they would be headed.
Invariably, it would be someone in a hurry,
   someone from out of town,
someone in distress,
   or all three wrapped into one.

Yesterday it was someone whose car had just been stolen
   and was trying to get to work on time, someone whose boyfriend
had just broken up with her leaving her downtown without a way home,
   someone trying to get to a rehearsal dinner on time
after arriving on a flight delayed for two hours,
   and someone who couldn't drive himself home
after an eye operation. Not that he had asked.

In the end, his job amounted to miles logged
   and fares accrued. But somehow
the cab became a confessional booth
   with the flow of words beginning sometimes before
the door had been pulled shut and trailing behind
   the person after the fare had been paid.

You must have nerves of steel, one passenger had said
   when they were snarled in a particularly bad traffic jam.
He was tempted to point out that the drama
   inside the cab often topped the chaos on the road,
but said nothing.
   Instead, he pictured himself relaxed
at home, lying on his side in front of his enormous TV
   with his top leg extending up to the ceiling,
his head propped up by his lower elbow and hand,
   the other hand gently holding the big toe of his lifted leg,
beholden to no one's directions but his own.

❖ *Anantāsana* (Side-Reclining Leg Lift)

Drifting Beyond Celsius, Fahrenheit

The weather forecaster looked under the sofa
   for his other shoe. He certainly couldn't announce
the percentage of expected precipitation on one foot.
   He eyed his cleats in the closet. Somehow they just didn't match
his three-piece suit. He wished he could pull his missing shoe
   out of the air, but magic was difficult at 4 a.m.

One day it would be someone else's job to give the 5 a.m. report
   and he would be able to eat a leisurely breakfast
of warm biscuits just as dawn tapered into morning.
   For now, a desire to be able to pay his mortgage was the glue
that kept the pieces of his schedule from falling apart.

He followed the lamp cord to the plug in the wall.
   Now how had his shoe gotten over there?
The blank look on his dog's face gave nothing away.
   With the hour hand now nearly quarter-to-five,
he forced himself to glide past the distractions—and focus,
   the way patience polishes stones into jewels.

After the noon forecast was complete, he headed home,
   his mind filled with Doppler radar reports, percentages
of precipitation, time-lapse maps showing fronts
   fast-forwarding across the country.
     Even after a year of the early shift,
he wasn't used to falling asleep while the sun still shone.
   It would take some time and slow stretches
     to loosen him into relaxation.

His dog watched him doing forward bends,
   backbends, extending his arms and tilting,
lying on his back with his legs in the air,
   until at last he sat down on the ground, cross-legged.
He turned to the right, placing his left hand on his right knee,
   right hand on the floor behind his right hip,
enjoying a gentle twist without going to his maximum.

At this point, his dog got up and went to her bed,

   knowing that after he repeated the twist on the other side,
the weary meteorologist would take *śavāsana* in bed,
   soon drifting beyond Celsius, Fahrenheit,
beyond anything any computer model could begin to predict.

    ❖ *Parivṛtta Sukhāsana* (Gentle Seated Twist)

The Allergist Who Was Allergic

The allergist who was allergic to any opinion but her own
    did not quite realize this.
Skilled as she was in identifying the problems of others,
    her own limitations were as invisible to her
as the microbes that rendered some of her patients miserable.
    As a result, she deftly avoided situations that would bring her
into direct contact with conflict.

Hypervigilant as a child who knows she is deathly allergic
    to peanuts or bee stings, she steered clear of conversations
when she knew they would be laced with views opposing her own.
    She did this so intuitively that she was not aware of her own avoidance,
further reinforcing her version of reality. Sometimes the world around her
    seemed to be folding into itself, not unlike origami,
ordinary stretches of time transforming into multiple dimensions
    without warning.

These changes left her feeling seasick,
    as if the solid ground beneath her
had turned into tumultuous waves.
    Why did anything have to change?
She herself was not immune,
    she observed, noting the new wrinkles
on the backs of her hands.

Winter had thawed into spring, and now it was early summer.
    The heavy rays of light wearied her,
making her prone to developing a rash,
    just as exposure to views antithetical to her own
inflamed her mind.

After her last patient had left and the last chart had been completed,
    she would head home to relax in a shaded area of the back patio
where, after sitting in meditation on a soft teal blanket,
    she'd lean back, lifting her legs, extending them straight ahead
so that her toes were eye level. She would then reach her arms forward,
    her body forming an abstract boat capable of remaining afloat,
even amidst life's unpredictable weathers.

        ❖ *Nāvāsana* (Boat Pose)

The Tattoo Artist

The tattoo artist took out her sketchpad and colored pens.
    After warming up with a few flowers
interwoven with a heart and a teardrop,
    she paused and asked herself the question
she pondered every day:
    What design
have I never seen before?

She closed her eyes.
    Darkness—and then a little flurrying
of light, like when the cable cuts out
    and the TV screen becomes snowy.
Surges of anxiety, frustration, despair—
    and then there it is: a configuration
arriving from some unknown place,
    some galaxy hidden within herself,
and she lingers there, hovering,
    memorizing each vibration of hue,
each thickness of each line,
    the shape of each curve,
until the design has fully imprinted itself
    in her consciousness. Her hand
begins to move. Intuitively,
    she re-creates the vision,
translating each nuance
    onto the page as if she is a scribe,
each flourish of her pen, reverent.

Hours later, she finishes, and blinks—
    as if waking from a dream.
She puts down her pen and paper
    and stands. After stretching her arms
and rotating her wrists,
    she bends her knees and lowers her hips.
Pressing her palms together,
    with ink-colored fingertips pointed upward,
she balances, her elbows pressing into her thighs
    as her thighs press back into her elbows,

the ball mounds of her feet tattooing themselves
   onto the soft earth, the twin design of her feet
impermanent as her breath, her pose, her work, this life.

      ❖ *Mālāsana* (Garland Pose/Squat)

Cages Dissolving

The zookeeper who counted her chickens
    before they hatched
was repeatedly disappointed
    when things did not turn out as expected:
When the two pandas
    did not mate. When the lone giraffe
became depressed. When the tiger paced
    obsessively in its cage.
When the monkeys began to ignore
    the hopeful faces pressed against the glass.
The more she tried to change
    the way the animals were acting,
the more exasperated she became.

After her last round for the day,
    she returned to her office, closed the blinds,
and sat down on the jungle-design carpet,
    stretching her legs out straight in front of her,
feet flexed, straightening her spine, sitting at attention,
    facing the wall in front of her
where a framed photo of herself in her twenties
    with the hairy arm of an orangutan around her shoulder
reminded her of why she had chosen this path.

Staring into her earlier eyes,
    she felt the savannah of choices
that had once spread before her.
    As she approached the bars that had caged her in
and gave them her full attention,
    she felt them beginning to dissolve,
opening up the space around her,
    her ribs suddenly no longer a prison for her heart.

        ❖ *Daṇḍāsana* (Staff Pose)

Ten Tiny Shields of Color

The perfectionistic pedicurist could not stand to see
   chips in the colored gloss of his toenails
when he lay on the ground with his legs up against a wall,
   making a perfect ninety-degree angle of himself.

"Well, why do you have to lie in that strange position
   anyway?" his co-workers would ask when he went on and on
about a miniscule chip in the purple or gray nail polish he loved.

Some even ventured to point out that leaving his toenails
   polish-free would solve the problem altogether.
He knew they were right, and yet he just couldn't
   let go of the way the ten tiny shields of color
on the tips of his toes pleased him,
   any more than he could let go of his evening ritual
of elevating his legs against the length of the wall
   of his salon after the Open light had been turned off.

Gradually, however, the more he accepted the paradox
   of remaining attentive while relaxing,
the more he found himself smiling
   as he trimmed and scrubbed and polished the nails
of the feet of those seated before him,
   listening to their dramas and dilemmas,
recognizing a tiny chip of himself in everything they said.

      ❖ *Viparīta-Karaṇī* (Legs-up-the-Wall Pose)

Blue Tulips with Forsythia

After two decades in the flower business,
   the florist was no longer surprised
by the unusual requests he received.

Blue tulips with forsythia one man had requested
   because, he said, the relationship has pretty much collapsed,
but there's always hope, right?
   This endnote was an invitation for the florist
to respond, to offer a bouquet of words
   to the burdened voice on the other end of the line.
Sir, how many blue tulips would you like, the florist replied,
   being much more comfortable with petals than platitudes.

Whether it was weddings or funerals,
   he liked to let the baby's breath speak for itself, allowing
the delicate white clusters to be interpreted freely.
   But when he got customers who gave him free rein—
oh, just put together something nice—it was as if his spirit grew
   from an amaryllis bulb to bloom in an instant.
The mixing and matching of mums, gladiolas, lilies,
   asters, snapdragons, roses, and whatever else he might have
made the air in the shop come alive.

And later, when the arrangements had been sent on their way
   and the floor swept free of leaves and stems,
he would often sit down, stretching his legs in front.
   Bending his right knee and taking his right foot over his left leg
so that the right foot touched the ground,
   he bent his left knee,
drawing his left foot toward his right hip.
   He paused and then stretched his left arm forward,
pressing his left elbow into the outside of his right knee.
   Then, turning to the right,
he threaded his left arm beneath his right knee
   and brought his right arm around his back, clasping his hands
together like floral ribbons forming a shimmering bow,
   the arrangement of his molecules feeling in balance at last.

❖   *Ardha Matsyendrāsana* (Half-Lord-of-the-Fishes Pose)

The Eraser Maker

The eraser maker could not avoid the irony
   that what he most wanted to erase
was far beyond stray marks on a page:
   the decisions that had seemed right at the time,
the brusquely spoken words now tattooed on someone's heart,
   the sent emails he could not begin to retrieve—
these and more were the unerasables that stalked him
   in the middle of the night, waking him, bleary-eyed,
at 2:13 a.m. or some other incomprehensible hour.

During the day, the steady focus on making erasers
   steadied him, liberating him
from the mental chatter of his worries.
   Pencil-top erasers, erasers for artists,
erasers with the emblems of companies—
   there was no shortage of requests,
even in the age of Backspace and Delete,
   for things to make other things disappear.

So after a long shift, a long week of long shifts,
   a long year of long weeks, he found himself
staring at the ceiling in the middle of the night
   once again. His cat meowed unappreciatively
as he dislodged her warm nest in the covers
   when he got out of bed and sat down on the floor.

As the cat curled up in the scoop of the pillow
   where his head had been,
he brought his palms and knees to the ground,
   rounding his spine toward the moon.
In this moment, he was inclined to believe that somewhere
   within the nano-technology of his breath,
he had the capacity
   to gently dissolve the regrets that marked him
with seemingly indelible ink.
   Slowly inhaling, he lowered his belly,
lifting his chin and tailbone, and as he exhaled,
   drawing his navel toward his spine,

lifting and rounding his back up to the sky,
    his breath caught a quiet flow, easing his mind,
removing the sludge of despair
    from his soul,
one cubic meter at a time.

      ❖ *Marjaryāsana/Bitilāsana* (Cat/Cow Pose)

The Xylophone Shop Musician

The pinging notes of C-D-E-F-G-A-B-C
   reverberated in the mind of the musician
long after he had turned off the lights
   and locked the door at the xylophone shop
where he spent his days. How he had ended up
   here instead of first chair in a premier symphony
was a story as ancient at the origins of music.
   The bassoon he played was not so far removed,
after all, from early instruments carved
   from hollowed branches. And wasn't it more
pleasing to watch customers as they sauntered in
   and wandered about, building up the courage
to hit the mallets against the metallic keys?

Something like light began to play around
   the edges of their eyes as sounds bloomed,
filling the air. Up and down the scale they went,
   faster and louder. It was only the rarest of customers
who ventured beyond, scrambling the notes
   into tiny songs. Or playing a single note
and pausing, savoring its nectar, its sweetness
   expanding mellifluously.

The shop owner passed the time
   making bets on which of the customers
would make a purchase. He was seldom correct.
   The rest of his time he spent fingering the notes
of his favorite concertos on the xylophone mallets
   he held in his hands trying to look busy
as he stood at the counter.

When he was certain no customers were in the shop,
   he bent his knees, lowering his hips, and raised his arms,
his fingers and palms pressing together.
   In this chairless chair, he sat as long as he could,
breathing deeply, mouth closed.
   Once, when he had his eyes closed, he heard a voice:

Are you stuck? A child had appeared, staring.
   Not unless I can't breathe, he had said
and vowed in that moment
   to keep his eyes from shutting out the world.

   ❖ *Utkaṭāsana* (Chair Pose)

Newly Ripe

The landscape artist thought the yard looked starved
    for a diagonal pattern. I could pour colored sand
to mark the contrast between the lawn and flowerbed,
    she mused. The idea teetered precariously against
the measure of her good judgment. As she sketched,
    her imagination favored curves like the ripples
in a cotton apron around a bustling cook.

No, she reconsidered, they're going to want angles.
    She only had to look at the sharp edges of the yard,
the house, and the roof for corroboration.
    What she could use right now was a cup of coffee.
Not only the jolt of caffeine, but the warmth of mahogany.

She stared up at the giant magnolia tree wedged
    between two dogwoods and wondered why
she hadn't been summoned ten years earlier
    before so much had already taken root.

Nevertheless, here she was, clearly needing to change
    the angle of her approach. Her father, an architect,
flashed into her mind—and what he did when he was stuck.

Ducking behind the glossy green of the magnolia,
    she stepped her feet apart, facing them to the right,
and extended her arms out wide, parallel to the earth.
    She took a deep breath. Swiveling to the right,
replacing her right arm with her left and taking her right arm behind,
    she leaned forward and down, positioning her left hand
on the outside of her right foot.
    Her right arm lifted to the sun, and as she concentrated
on not tipping over, her mind cleared like a freshly tilled yard,
    free from any weeds, any superimposed designs,
newly ripe for something, anything to sprout.

    ❖ *Parivṛtta Trikoṇāsana* (Revolved Triangle)

Galloping

The hippotherapist greeted her client with a warm hello,
    the mane of her chestnut hair glistening.
As the client hoisted himself up on the horse,
    he seemed lighter, as if suddenly
he was no longer saddled by his speech impediment
    and the unpredictable locomotions of his limbs.

He sat tall, his spine straight, as if his shoulders
    had forgotten how to slump.
It was as though the vibration of the steady gleam,
    the calm posture of the horse had entered into his cells,
bathing his hippocampus in golden light.

He looked at her expectantly, ready to take on the world.
    If she had not witnessed transformations
like this repeatedly, she, too,
    would have questioned the validity of this technique.

Even now, there was no way to quantify the radiance in the client
    to researchers. The muscle-memory
of the soothing pelvic rocking of the horse's gentle motion
    did not translate into numbers
as easily as it realigned neural pathways.

It was like when she did her forward bends
    in front of the stables each morning, swimming her arms down
as she folded forward and sweeping them into a wide wingspan
    as she rose.
Along the way, the flaring nostrils of her stress subsided,
    preparing her to rein in the various crises galloping
into the back-to-back appointments of her day.

        ❖ *Uttānāsana* (Forward Fold)

A Potential Hiccup

The wedding planner was used to watching
   the weather reports. But he still wasn't used to watching
the virus reports. Were gatherings limited to ten, fifty,
   or one hundred this week? He couldn't decide which was worse—
the threat of a thunderstorm or the chance of losing
   Wi-Fi connection for the livestream of the ceremony,
family scattered and stranded all over the world,
   tuning in on Zoom, typing the meeting code and password
into phones and tablets with excited, forlorn fingers—
   thrilled to attend and dejected not to be there in person.
At least he wasn't a caterer, he reminded himself—
   the orders for hors d'oeurves and specialty cuisine
for rehearsal dinners and wedding galas
   gone by the wayside during these masked months of lockdown.
Though matrimonial business had plummeted,
   the fact that he still had a job assuaged somewhat
the annoyance of having to remain in professional mode
   all day—never knowing when a client would video-call
to go over "one last detail" for the millionth time.
   Still, this was their big day—their (hopefully) once-in-a-lifetime
matrimony, and so he rose to the occasion, day after day,
   diving deeper into his well of compassion
as anxiety levels in brides and grooms escalated.

After a particularly draining call about a potential hiccup
   in the bridal bouquet delivery or the performance
of Pachelbel's Canon, he liked to find his way
   to hands and knees and pause there with his fingers spread wide,
feeling the security of the ground beneath him—
   his back parallel to the floor, becoming a table, stable and steady.
Internally scanning, he observed the left side of his body from left heel to crown
   and then travelled down the right side from crown to right heel,
breathing into the center, uniting his two halves—
   first scanning the front of his body from navel to crown
and then the upper back body, breathing into the back of his heart.
   Next, he scanned the lower body, his internal gaze gliding from the navel
slowly to the tops of his feet, and then from the soles up to the calves,
   thighs, and sacrum, back to his core. Just like all the wedding tables

that had been decorated and dismantled through the years,
   he was expendable, temporary, too. Breathing into this truth somehow freed him, calming him, giving him the strength to rise again.

> ❖ *Bhārmanāsana* (Table Pose)

In the Conference Room

The administrative assistant was alone in the conference room
   lying on her back on the carpet, shoes off, thanking the 2% spandex
of her pantsuit for allowing her to stretch comfortably,
   first bringing her knees to her chest and hugging them,
then releasing one leg back down to the ground and straightening it
   while extending the other leg up toward the fluorescent lights.

Looping her thumb and first finger around the toe
   inside her lifted nyloned foot, she slowly released the foot
out to the side, moving her leg towards the floor.

It was precisely at the moment that she felt
   the tightness in her hips and low back ease
that she realized she was not alone.
   Through the door she had shut had appeared
her boss who, as she had assured herself
   when checking his schedule three times,
was not due back from his lunch meeting
   for another hour.

As a planner, a scheduler, and a detail aficionado,
   little slipped past her,
until now, splayed out as she was without a word
   of sense coming to her rescue,
her boss retreating
   in the same surreal way he had appeared,
as if she were dreaming.

Blink. Blink.
   No, there was no doubt about it. She was fully awake.
She would have to put on her shoes
   and stride back out to her post smiling,
resuming her at-attention position
   in her leather chair with wheels,
but not without first switching legs in her stretch,
   balancing out the right with the left,
making her gaffe
   perfectly symmetrical,
if nothing else.

❖ *Supta-Pādāṅguṣṭhāsana* (Reclining Hand-to-Big-Toe Pose)

In the Sweetness of Pre-Dawn

In the sacred sweetness of pre-dawn,
   the social worker climbed down from his bed,
found a cross-legged position
   on his meditation cushion,
placed his palms facing up on his thighs,
   tip of his thumb and index finger in contact,
elbows wide, and began exhaling forcefully,
   the bellows breath spreading warmth
throughout his being.

Then, as he began pumping his abdomen
   with the quicker cleansing breaths
of a skull-shining breath, he felt his mind clear.

Next came the balancing breath,
   alternating inhalations and exhalations
through left and right nostrils,
   bringing his solar and lunar energies
into equilibrium.

To nourish his calm, with his hands cupped over his eyes,
   elbows wide, he began humming as he exhaled,
thumbs closing off the flaps of his ears,
   the soft vibrations of sound soothing
even his most frayed nerve.

Bathing his being with these cleansing breaths
   was the only way he felt able to face another day
of home visits where he would see and hear things
   he'd have wished he hadn't—
     children in volatile situations or being neglected,
   addicts refusing to enter treatment programs,
and more.

He came back to his breath,
   following the inhale, following the exhale,
tracing the inner pathways
   to the oasis of peace within,
and lingered.

❖ *Prāṇāyāma* (Breathwork)

The Marshmallow Shop

The manager of the marshmallow shop was at his wits' end.
   It seemed that no one was satisfied anymore.
Instead of monthly specials,
   customers now expected weekly ones.

Three years ago, when he first opened,
   just having marshmallows shaped like the political candidates,
sports mascots, and Dora the Explorer had been enough
   to put him on the map.
Entire families walked in out of sheer curiosity
   and walked out, each smiling with a sugary designer treat.

Your job is all fluff, his brother, a broker, chided
   at the once-a-year holiday gatherings,
and so the marshmallow manager,
   though he certainly had no desire
for his brother's definition of success,
   decided to challenge himself to something more.

So he dove into flavors. He started simply enough:
   chocolate, cinnamon, cherry and worked himself up
to mint chocolate chip and caramel cappuccino.

Those were the good ole days of a flavor a month.
   Customers were content with the choice of a dish of miniatures
or a larger slice tucked in a waxpaper pocket
   dusted with a glittery shine.
      That was before the hybrids—
pomegranate avocado, root beer hot pepper,
   onion lavender, and the like,
all the way to high-end requests
   like rose saffron and Godiva gold.

Where did people come up with these ideas
   he wanted to know, and should he stick to natural coloring
even if that meant cloudy gray or a dingy chartreuse?
   These were the kind of questions that kept him up at night.
That, and his wife's snoring.

    2 a.m. usually found him
  slipping out of bed and onto the floor where he lay
with his legs up the wall, creating a right angle of himself,
    and if he stayed there long enough, things seemed to come into balance,
even if it was just the slowing of his mind, the easing of his breath.

        ❖ *Viparīta Karaṇī* (Legs-up-the-Wall Pose)

Eyes and Ears Alert

He straightened his uniform, secured his radio and gun,
    and said the rosary.
This had been his morning ritual before he started his shift
    for as long as he could recall.
His mother, who often urged him to work a desk job,
    needed him to come back from his shift alive.
Try as he might to reassure her that his days patrolling the perimeter
    as a security guard were largely uneventful
they both knew that in any split-second this could change.

So he kept his eyes and ears alert,
    noticing what slipped by most people
without a second thought:
    how this person paused or laughed,
the vacant gaze in another,
    the tightened jaw in someone else.
Over and over, he rehearsed in his mind
    what he would do in a vast array of scenarios.

The long hours on his feet gave him time to ponder,
    exploring passageways in his mind
even as his eyes and ears remained on high alert.
    Occasionally, when the coast was clear,
he'd bend his knee, lift his foot,
    and hold the steel toe of his boot,
    extending his leg out in front for several breaths,
and then out to the side, seeing if he could keep his balance.
    Then he'd try it on the other side
before coming back to Mountain Pose,
    both feet on the cement,
ready, at a moment's notice,
    to break into a sprint.

❖ *Utthita-Hasta-Pādāṅguṣṭhāsana* (Standing Hand-to-Big-Toe Pose)

The Shoeshiner

It can't be a shop if it doesn't have walls,
    his buddies would tease him,
mostly to take the focus off the fact
    that they didn't have jobs at all.
At least that's what he told himself
    as yet another frequent flyer stepped up
into one of his chairs in the busy terminal
    and, while still carrying on a conversation
with whomever was on the other side
    of the cell phone,
nodded to him
    to request a shine.

If only he could shine
    what could not be seen.
Mortal as he was,
    he began polishing the leather
housing the feet
    temporarily taking up residence
in his shop on their journey
    between points A and B.

It seemed the shoes had begun talking to him lately,
    or maybe he was just getting better
at listening. Paying attention. Some shoes
    had just about had it, worn nearly ragged
by too much this and that. Others were ready
    to take on the world, their soles not yet flattened
by endless impressions and progressions.

After a full eight hours of scrubbing,
    polishing, and shining, he'd had his fill of shoes.
Upon reaching his doorstep,
    off came his shoes and socks, his bare feet
greeting the cement, the carpet, the tile floor.
    Later, he would sit with his knees wide apart,
his legs folded into butterfly wings,
    the soles of his feet touching,

his hands wrapping around his valiant feet,
    the feet that had carried him,
most auspiciously,
    most devotedly,
 home.

          ❖ *Baddha-Koṇāsana* (Bound Angle Pose)

The Sky Ablaze

It was fire season. Again. And the sky was ablaze
   with an eerie orange glow thick with smoke.
The firefighter prepared to walk once more
   into the dragon's mouth of conflagration.

Why she had chosen this path
   had everything to do with losing a friend to arson
and something to do with the call to action
   she had always felt each time she heard
the fire engines' sirens screaming down the city streets.

She kept her lungs strong throughout the year,
   moving through twelve *sūrya namaskārs* each morning,
welcoming the sun's warmth into her heart.

But this fire season was unprecedented.
   She felt her bronchial wings struggling
in a way they never had before. For the first time
   she understood asthma
as her lungs heaved and sputtered,
   as she choked and coughed out the toxic air.

Glass was melting in the 3000-degree heat
   and rocks were being pulverized.
Computer keyboards had been burnt to a crisp
   and entire homes were now rubble.
Never had so many fires burned
   or ignited so many acres at once.

Once she entered the flow she didn't want to stop
   until every last flame was vanquished,
but down time was being strictly enforced—
   so once she had removed the layers of her gear,
she sat quietly, letting her system recalibrate,
   following her in-breath, following her out-breath,
bringing her tongue gently between
   upper teeth and lower teeth
broadening her mouth into a smile,

inhaling through the corners of her mouth
and exhaling, mouth closed, through her nose,
feeling a cool tranquility spreading slowly
across the scorched terrain of her mind.

❖ *Śitkāri* (Cooling Breath)

Divinely Designed Lungs

The minister removed his suit coat and tie,
   loosened the collar of his button-down shirt,
removed the cufflinks from his wrists,
   and reflected on his flock.

Some in the congregation were so hot-headed,
   complaining about the smallest changes
implemented into the Sunday service,
   and others he had to light a fire beneath
to get them to attend or to say two words.

The rest sat somewhere between the two
   on a pew in his mind—unpredictable
as the weather in this rural place
   where he had agreed to move
without realizing what he was getting himself into.

Oh, every community had its issues—
   he'd seen that in the past three decades
from the pulpit, by the bedsides, at the funerals and weddings,
   in prayer requests whispered into his ear.

But this place was different. It seemed even the sun struggled
   to find its way through the large stained-glass window
portraying Christ on the cross.
   In moments like these, as he tried to remember
why he'd chosen ministry over an MBA,
   he sat down, closing his mouth, and pressed his right thumb
against his right nostril and inhaled deeply.
   At the end of the inhale, he closed off his left nostril
with his right ring finger and exhaled, surrendering,
   letting go—
then he drew a fresh inhale through his right nostril
   before closing off the right nostril and exhaling
slowly through the left—

This purification, this nourishment of God-given breath
   flowing through divinely designed lungs,

   was like the Lord's Supper to him,
a sacred ritual
     balancing him, renewing him,
        making him, once again, whole.

❖ *Anuloma Viloma* (Alternate Nostril Breath)

Masking Her Shock

The newscaster blinked at the words
    scrolling across the teleprompter…
With years of training in masking her shock,
    her mouth was able to deliver the breaking news
with measured inflection rather than gasps and shouts.
    Living in a city nearly eaten alive
by drug abuse and nepotism,
    she was used to a fair amount of seismic reports,
but this particular year planetary pent-up storms
    had been unleashed in fire, flood, treachery, and treason,
devastating the very equilibrium of society, knocking lives
    sideways and upside-down. How was it that she,
in whom anxiety rode bareback at all hours of night and day,
    was supposed to be the calm voice and face
that millions turned to in their isolated states to find comfort?

If she didn't get some sleep soon,
    make-up was no longer going to be able to hide
the bags beneath her eyes.
    But with a new drama breaking every hour,
how could she drift into dreamland?

Sometimes if she did some stretching,
    she could soothe herself to sleep—
at least for a while. She unrolled her mat and stepped onto it,
    transporting herself from the speed of newsfeeds
to the slow rhythm of her breath
    gradually lengthening the exhale
to twice that of the inhale.
    As she flowed from one posture to another,
she lingered now and then on her favorites.
    Kneeling on the ground, she stretched her arms forward
on the mat into Child's Pose. Then, coming briefly to Table position,
    she glided her hips forward, easing them down to the mat.
Coming to a full stretch of her arms, with palms pressing into the mat,
    she lifted her legs slightly, the tops of her feet pressing into the floor.
And with her chest expanding, heart opening,

shoulder blades drawing in, throat opening, she deepened her breath, becoming, in that moment,
    upward-facing to the mystical light of the moon.

> ❖ *Ūrdhva-Mukha-Śvānāsana* (Upward-Facing Dog)

Beyond Coupons

As the next customer began to unload his groceries
    onto the conveyor belt, she noticed the mix
of healthy cheese puffs, the tubs of sugar-free, dairy-free,
    gluten-free ice cream, the fresh organic vegetables,
and the bottles of vitamins and supplements
    beside the chocolate fudge brownies.
She pictured him snacking as he burned the midnight oil
    to meet deadlines from an unforgiving boss,
and then jolting awake by a 5 a.m. alarm on his phone, pausing
    to take one of each of his eleven supplements before running out the door.

The repetition of scanning items and taking payments got old quickly
    and her spirit started to sour after weighing one too many citrus fruits
or asking one too many customers if their day was going well.
    Little did she know that for some of her customers
her "Have a nice day!" she called out with a smile
    was the only good wish they received that day.
On long days, observing the combinations of items
    and listening to the stories they told kept her sane.
Still, her feet hurt and her shoulders ached.

When she got home and showered off all the supermarket air,
    she was ready to relax. She rested in table pose
with knees and palms touching the ground, her back parallel to the earth.
    Then, lifting her right palm off the ground, turning her torso to the right,
        she swept her right arm up to the sky on an inhale,
    and then, exhaling slowly, she lowered her arm, sliding it across
the floor to the left, her right cheek and shoulder touching down
    before inhaling as her right arm began retracing its arc
back up to the sky. She then paused in Table and repeated the movement fluidly
    on the other side. Moving in this way, far from coupons and weekly specials,
she felt her grace, her sanctity, her true nature
    slowly beginning to return, like a dear friend.

      ❖ *Pārśva-Bālāsana* (Revolved Child Pose/Thread-the-Needle)

Into the Beehive

He paused for a moment before stepping into the beehive—
   that's what the electronics store felt like to him.
Throughout his eight-hour shift, the voices
   of anxious, excited, and frustrated customers
buzzed through the air.
   There was nothing like a major purchase
to spike the blood pressure,
   and nothing like a phone or computer malfunctioning
to bring out the worst in people.

Part of his training, therefore, had been akin
   to crisis management: maintain eye contact,
nod, be an ally, be part of the solution.
   And so when they asked him about a certain feature
of a certain model of a certain mobile phone
   nine different times in nine different ways,
he remained clear and calm, vowing
   not to be derailed by the chaotic surges
of energy around him.

But after fielding the many questions,
   troubleshooting like a super sleuth,
and soothing customers
   freaked out by cracked screens,
digital systems gone awry,
   and photos gone missing,
his nerves jangled and tangled,
   and he found himself dreaming of a massage.

With a family of five waiting for him at home, though,
   there was no time for that. So when he got in his car
instead of turning on the ignition, he placed his hands
   on his lap, palms face up, closed his eyes,
bent his index fingers toward his palms,
   wrapping his thumbs around his index fingers,
hugging them. Sitting like this for a good five or ten minutes
   calmed him down enough to where he was able to drive home
without overreacting to the traffic or angrily honking his horn,

with space in his mind and heart opening
to embrace fully his family
 and all that mattered most.

> ❖ *Vāyu Mudrā* (Hand Position for Air Element)

Inside a Pocket of a Sci-Fi Film

Just six months ago he was on the fast track,
   skipping rungs on the corporate ladder
as he swiftly climbed—
   and now, a furlough and a downsizing later,
he was working inside a virtual structure
   he didn't even know existed before.
He was like a stealth pilot flying a large machine
   and it was his duty to watch all the panels,
making sure the CEOs remained airborne
   with as little turbulence as possible.

He was not to be seen or heard, muting and unmuting,
   spotlighting and pinning, sharing screens, managing conferences online,
and tactfully notifying in the best steward's voice he could summon
   when a board member or committee member had a virtual hand raised
or an unanswered question was pending in the chat.

He was also there to fend off the intruders
   who tried from time to time to interrupt, intercept,
or vandalize the slides using the annotation drawing tools.
   (Had he really earned a graduate degree for this?)
Nevertheless, it was his duty and his duty alone
   to make sure meetings were recorded
and that the recordings were properly saved and archived.

Days, weeks, months were zooming past.
   Had he fallen into a pocket of a sci-fi film?
Pay attention: there's a new chat message
   and it's almost time to assign breakout rooms.

After a full day of having his eyes glued to the screen,
   he loved to rub his palms together and cup them gently over his eyes.
Then, to calm his nerves, he took his index fingers
   to the center of his forehead, his thumbs to the flaps of his ears,
and let his other fingers softly cradle his eyes.

Keeping his spine long, with sit bones rooted into his chair,
   elbows wide, chin slightly tucked, he inhaled deeply through his nose

and began humming on the exhale,
   sending subtle soothing vibrations throughout his body
from the crown of his head to the tips of his toes,
   the resonance of peace radiating inside each of his cells
more powerfully than the dynamic force of any electromagnetic wave.

❖ *Bhramarī Prāṇāyāma* (Bumblebee Breath)

The Unthinkable Backbend of the Sky's Deep Blue

It wasn't so much the fact that the clocks were running
   backwards that alarmed the wizard. The rust forming
on the coils in the calligraphic script of ancient words
   bothered him more. With the ancient language becoming scarce
and with the nomadic turns his memory had taken lately,
   the illuminated texts of sacred stories were moving
toward the magnet of oblivion.

To compound the situation,
   his sleeps were becoming factories for the strangest dreams
and even if he had known the process of batik painting
   he still could not have replicated the intricate textured layers
of his dreams. The library of his mind was drowning
   volume by volume in the dazzle of spider webs in sunlight,
in the unthinkable backbend of the sky's deep blue,
   and in the bright orange blaze of autumn leaves.

If tomorrow is a new day, said the wizard, stroking his long silver beard,
   then the stars will give us another chance to hear their songs,
and we will have another chance to understand.
   But for now, he said, smoothing his purple gown
embroidered with the sun and moon, I must set myself free.

And with that, he crouched down and, gingerly balancing,
   placed his knees securely upon his upper arms, and then,
as if remembering something nested deep in his cellular consciousness,
   he leaned forward, lifting his feet and paused,
as if any minute he might conjure a spell
   for wings and remove the need
for his hands or feet to touch the floor.

                ❖ *Bakāsana* (Crow Pose)

The Frazzled Hairstylist

The frazzled hairstylist felt increasingly flattened
   by the weight of her clients' lives. They came in,
one after another, chatting about doomsday,
   cataloguing the crises in their personal lives
as if there were no tomorrow. A captive audience,
   she found herself trying to cut and style
more quickly, sending the newly coiffed
   on their way so that she could catch her breath
before the next customer arrived, worried
   about a spouse's indifference or the capsized economy
more than his or her own negative outlook
   leaking into the atmosphere like aerosol fumes.
Even a country music station
   offered more uplifting stories than her clients
whose voices had once beamed with highlights
   of their most recent vacations or shopping sprees.

As she saw her own tired eyes reflected
   in the floor-length mirrors, she felt
how much her high-heeled feet ached
   and how much she longed to be at home
inverted into a headstand, her hair fanning out
   in a circle on the floor, the soles of her feet
facing the ceiling, her body balanced
   as a freestanding column,
the heaviness
   of her day dissipating, her despair
turned on its head.

          ❖ *Śīrṣāsana* (Headstand Pose)

As the Colors Bloomed

After getting all of the cattle into the pen,
   the rancher pulled the loose strands of her hair behind her ears
and wiped the sweat from her face. Working sun-up to sundown
   didn't leave much time for anything else.

She was hard-pressed to keep up with bills, laundry,
   and making a few homecooked meals every now and then.
How her cousins in the city had time
   to go to concerts and yoga classes was beyond her.
With the hours she spent hauling feed and rounding up stock,
   her muscles were perfectly toned.

"You don't even need stress relief,"
   they would say, "being in nature all the time and all that."
It was true—she fared better with open skies than cubicles,
   but that didn't erase her financial fears,
and the vet bills kept rising.

On nights when she couldn't sleep,
   she'd go out and gaze up at the stars.
On sleepless nights when the rain poured down,
   she'd pull out the book of mandala designs
and the pack of 100 colored pencils
   her cousins had sent at the holidays last year:
as the colors slowly bloomed in the shapes
   of the circular patterns, she felt peace in the symmetry
as she moved beyond her day-to-day tasks
   toward the center of the design
while simultaneously moving toward the center of herself,
   a wordless internal location GPS could not begin to define.

❖ *Maṇḍala* Meditation

Excavating

Somewhere along his twenty-three-year career,
   the archeologist had started rising before dawn
to move through a series of postures and stretches
   in peace and quiet before the rest of the household awoke.

Placing his hands by his shoulders, he lifted himself up
   from the floor from prone position with the strength of his arms,
extending his legs behind him, curling his toes under.
   Facing the ground, his gaze went through the carpet and floorboards
into the earth, imagining what he would find
   in a dig there on his own property.

In traveling the world, he'd found his share of exquisite shards of pottery
   and even fully intact relics on multiple continents,
many of the items he'd unearthed now displayed in museums.

It was a strange feeling peeling back the veils of time, never knowing
   what would be revealed by upturning one more scoop of earth.
"Let bygones be bygones" and "let sleeping dogs lie," people would say,
   but he couldn't help but believe he'd been put on this earth
to help piece together the mysteries of the past.

Along the way, he found himself slowly excavating buried memories
   from his youth, some more welcome than others.
As the sun started to rise, the painted cross
   that he'd brought back from South America caught the light
from where it hung on the wall and gleamed,
   his signal that it was time—
time to prepare for whatever he would uncover today:
   in the ground, in his files, in his research,
or inside the contours
   of the ever-mystifying internal terrain
inside the depths of his own mind.

             ❖ *Phalakāsana* (Plank Pose)

The Perfection of Imperfection

He loved his job. He loved every part: the joy he felt
   when he found a typo, especially a subtle one
that the spellchecker would miss,
   the frustration he felt when errors slipped past him,
the camaraderie he felt with some of his co-workers,
   the competitiveness he felt with others,
experiencing all of this without reaching,
   without grasping for something else.

After spending the first twelve years
   of his working life complaining,
both aloud and in the internal chambers of his mind,
   always wanting things to be different than they were,
he'd been forced to revise.
   An ulcer and four years of therapy later,
he had let go of seeing the world around him
   as if it needed his edits.

Part of it was realizing
   that none of it could be perfect—
his job, his life, the drafts
   of newspaper articles he reviewed—
and sitting with that:
   sitting in the middle of the imperfection,
breathing out as much as he was breathing in,
   at home in the bittersweetness—
the perfection of imperfection
   exquisite in its endless revisions,
its utter unfixableness,
   the sacredness
of its inevitable surrender.

            ❖ *Aparigraha* (Non-grasping)

The Unemployment Agency

There were always at least three people waiting in the phone queue
    of the helpline at the unemployment agency—and sometimes fifteen,
or fifty during peak periods. The technical glitches he could usually resolve,
    but how to come to terms with the tales they told continued to elude him.

There were those who were filing for the first time
    after three decades of being gainfully employed—
and those who could not collect a penny
    falling just shy of the income cutoff by ten dollars—
earning a few hundred per week for working hard
    while others, free to relax at the park or to watch sitcoms,
drew more than a thousand. Others told of working with excellence
    and dedication for decades without any wage increase for years of service,
while others told of being let go for reasons undisclosed.

The shame, the hurt, the outrage, confusion they felt was palpable,
    as well as their fear, their dismay at not being able to make ends meet,
their degrees and years of experience somehow no longer offering a safety net
    with the job market teeming now with applicants.

As he listened, his heart melted, his mind opened,
    as he saw that with a reshuffling of the deck
he could just as easily be the one phoning in for help—
    and with that realization, he searched deeply within
for a compassionate reply,
    one that would ease the suffering
and restore a sense of humanity,
    honoring the sacredness of the human being
on the other end of the line.

        ❖ *Karuṇā* (Compassion)

The Vast Cosmos

The barking, the howling, the whimpering, the mewing—
    she could not erase from the soundtracks of her mind.
Sometimes she heard them in the night,
    though her home was thirty miles away from the animal shelter,
their voices etched into the audioscape of her dreams.

Joy sang in her heart when one of these abandoned four-footeds was chosen,
    adopted into a chance for survival; these miracles kept her going
and offset the gut-wrenching punch of others being euthanized,
    the space of the shelter limited and the number of adoptions always in flux.

And then there were the days people returned a dog or cat that they had adopted,
    like a pair of shoes or a sweatsuit that didn't quite fit. Times were hard,
and pet food and bills added up. There had to be some divine order
    to all of this, she thought as she did her daily walk-through, some of the dogs
wagging their tails with hope, others cowering into the corners of their cages,
    the cats seemingly meditating upon each of their nine lives.

Back in her office, overwhelmed
    by the limitations of funding with the clock ticking,
realizing there was only so much she could do,
    she began to pay attention to the flow of her breath
and let her attention rest at the crown of her head,
    acknowledging all that existed beyond herself,
feeling her connection with the vast cosmos,
    visualizing a glimmering thousand-petaled lotus
blessed equally by the light of the sun and the moon.

        ❖ *Sahasrāra Cakra* (Crown Chakra)

The Collective Sanctuary

Amidst the swirl of relocating his broker business to the home front
    in the midst of his wife homeschooling their kindergartener and pre-teens,
he often felt called to step outside the world beneath their roof,
    shoveling the driveway of a homebound neighbor
or moving the newspaper from the curb to the doorstep
    of neighbors in their eighties or nineties.
Not mentioning to anyone how he'd helped
    sweetened it for him somehow,
like making an anonymous donation
    placed in the offering plate
of the collective sanctuary of life.

Other times he'd go online and choose a few GoFundMe accounts
    to support anonymously, crowdsourcing the causes that spoke to his soul
or donating through PayPal links at Zoom concerts of folksingers
    or to non-profits livestreaming events online.

While even his financial dexterity and good intentions
    could not eradicate poverty, injustice, violence, or apathy,
he could offer his best from his heart—daily,
    with hope, like a coin tossed, shining,
into a wishing well ever-widening
    in a world somehow out of tune
with the hymn of love
    woven into its sacred core.

        ❖ *Sevā* (Service)

Silent Victory

The delivery person placed another tower of boxes
   on her dolly and wheeled them up to the door.

Who would order seven different things at one time?
   It was not her place to speculate, her boss would say,
but she was curious. Curiosity killed the cat, as the saying goes,
   but she was not a cat, though nothing could stop the dogs
from barking each time she rang the bell.

She hated ringing the bell, but how could she not?
   It was part of her job, and with all of the doorbell security cameras now,
she had to remind herself her movements were not unseen.
   It could wear on a person—never getting to open any of the packages—
large or small—and the weight of them all!
   No worry: even though she no longer had time to go to the gym,
her muscles were stronger than ever.

With people ordering more and more items, requests to work overtime
   came pouring in. It was tempting—and yet she knew she needed rest.
When she had completed her last delivery of the day,
   she would pause right there in the parking lot, plant her feet,
bend her knees, sit down in a richly embroidered invisible chair,
   and shoot her arms skyward in silent victory.

She was fierce. She would not be vanquished.
   And the way her thighs talked to her
in this moment reassured her
   that yes, she *would* make it through
another day, another week, another year—
   and beyond!

              ❖ *Utkaṭāsana* (Chair Pose)

The Final Relaxation

Lying on his back at the end of yoga class
   in the final relaxation, the travel agent felt tears
coming to his eyes. For years, he had watched:
   helping people plan their trips across the country
and across the world—to ranches in Montana,
   to luaus in Hawaii, to Swiss chalets,
and to meditation retreats in Japan—
   and yet where had he been? To the office,
the supermarket, home, and back again
   in an endless loop. The teacher was saying something
about letting go, relaxing into the impermanence,
   trusting the ground to hold them.

In that moment, he saw his bones turning into ash, following
   thousands or millions climbing the divine staircase
to the world beyond as their bodies burned beside the Ganges.
   Then he began seeing his bones tucked inside the ground
in the mountains where his forefathers and foremothers had slept
   for centuries, each one having exhaled themselves
from the confines of this life into the great beyond.

"If the mind wanders, come back to the breath,"
   he heard the teacher advising as if she had a front seat view
of his mind. "Lengthen your exhale," she was saying,
   and he did his best to do so, dying a bit with each exhalation,
each surrendering giving birth to an abundance of breath
   revitalizing, renewing, restoring
a seemingly boundless flow of peace within.

        ❖ *Śavāsana* (Corpse Pose)

References

Bachman, Nicolai. *The Language of Yoga*. Boulder, CO: Sounds True, 2004.

Lad, Vasant and Anisha Durve. *Marma Points of Ayurveda: The Energy Pathways for Healing Body, Mind, and Consciousness with a Comparison to Traditional Chinese Medicine.* Albuquerque, NM: The Ayurvedic Press. 2008.

Acknowledgements

I extend my deep appreciation for the prior publications of the poems in this collection listed below:

"The Cuckoo Clock Repair Shop" in *The Threepenny Review* (2012) and in *Breath, Bone, Earth, Sky* (Finishing Line Press, 2014)

"The Plant Waterer Who Speaks Six Languages" in *Poet Lore* (2012)

"Stronger Than Concrete and Lighter Than Air" in *Atlanta Review* (2006) and in *Faces on the Metro* {in a modified form as "The Construction Worker"}

"The Ladder of the Spine" in *Potomac Review* (2006) {in a modified form as "The Tollbooth Collector"}

"The Tripled Tempo" in *Harpur Palate* (2004) and in *Faces on the Metro* {in a modified form as "The Musician"}

"In the Dissonance" in *Eureka Literary Literary Magazine* (2005) and in *Faces on the Metro* {in a modified form as "The Organist"}

~~

Thank you to *Bosque Journal* for awarding the following five poems the Editor's Prize for Poetry in 2016:

"The Dazzles of Their 'Fine'" in *Bosque* (2016) {with the title "The Bank Teller"}

"The Gentlest Arrow" in *Bosque* (2016) {with the title "The Professional Oboist"}

"The Groomer Who Was Once a Cat" in *Bosque* (2016)

"Death-in-Life" in *Bosque* (2016) {with the title "The Groundskeeper"}

"Fermata" in *Bosque* (2016) {with the title "The Conductor"}

~~

"Swimming without Swimming" in *Bosque* (2018) {with the title "The Oceanographer Who Could Not Swim"}

"Circuitry Within" in *Bosque* (2018) {with the title "The Interpreter"}

"On the Cusp" in *Faces on the Metro* (Pudding House Press, 2005) {in a modified form as "The Artist"}

"Inside the Gaping Unknown" in *Faces on the Metro* (Pudding House Press, 2005) {in a modified form as "The Bachelor"}

"His Plan to Save the World" in *Faces on the Metro* (Pudding House Press, 2005) {in a modified form as "The Beggar"}

"Reverse Ransom" in *Faces on the Metro* (Pudding House Press, 2005) {in a modified form as "The Burglar"}

"Diamond of Lentils" in *Eleven A.M.* (Wildflower Press, 2003) in a modified form as "Curvature of Air" and in *Faces on the Metro* (Pudding House Press, 2005) {in a modified form as "The Chef"}

"In These Quiet Hours" in *Faces on the Metro* (Pudding House Press, 2005) {in a modified form as "The Drycleaner"}

"Polynomials Popping into Her Mind" in *Faces on the Metro* (Pudding House Press, 2005) {in a modified form as "The Engineer"}

"The Unsolved Case" in *Faces on the Metro* (Pudding House Press, 2005) {in a modified form as "The FBI Agent"}

"Proud as a Peacock" in *Faces on the Metro* (Pudding House Press, 2005) {in a modified form as "The Journalist"}

"Small Globes" in *Faces on the Metro* (Pudding House Press, 2005) {in a modified form as "The Ophthalmologist"}

"Lunar Luminosity" in *Faces on the Metro* (Pudding House Press, 2005) {in a modified form as "The Seamstress"}

"Catapulted to Stardom" in *Faces on the Metro* (Pudding House Press, 2005) {in a modified form as "The Security Guard"}

"The Toy Maker" in *Faces on the Metro* (Pudding House Press, 2005) {in a modified form as "The Toy Maker"}

"At the Carnival of Humanity" in *Faces on the Metro* (Pudding House Press, 2005) {in a modified form as "The Waitress"}

~Gratitude~

Thank you, yoga, for being, at times, my poetry, and thank you, poetry, for being, at times, my yoga. Both of you are sacred companions to me in this life.

An ocean of appreciation to India—the homeland of yoga—and to all who have helped pass down the teachings of yoga through the ages.

A deep bow of gratitude to all of my teachers of writing and yoga through the many years and to my students who, for decades, have taught me something new every day.

Thank you to *The Threepenny Review* for accepting my very first yoga poem in this series back in 2012 just days after I submitted it, a tremendous unexpected blessing that inspired me to write more.

Thank you to Pudding House Press for publishing (back in 2005) my chapbook *Faces on the Metro*, my first exploration of work-based poems, from which some of the poems in this collection grew.

Thank you to Chatter Albuquerque for inviting me to read my poems as a Spoken Word Artist—and for the audience member who purchased my chapbook *Breath, Bone, Earth, Sky* specifically for "The Cuckoo Clock Repair Shop." This reminded me of the family of related yoga poems that had accumulated and encouraged me to dust them off back in 2016.

Thank you, Hilda Raz and *Bosque Journal*, for awarding five of these poems *Bosque*'s Editor's Prize in 2016, inspiring me to explore this path further.

Many thanks to all who read drafts, with special thanks to Karen Dunlop, Patrick Houlihan, Gloria Drayer, and Jeanne Shannon for their time, care, and feedback in reviewing the manuscript in full.

Much gratitude to Finishing Line Press for giving this family of poems a good home and to editor Christen Kincaid for excellent editorial support.

Thank you, Dr. Edwin G. Wilson and Dr. Tom O. Phillips of Wake Forest University, and author Howard E. Cummins of Appalachia, Virginia, for believing in my writing and in me all of these years.

Deep appreciation to my teacher, Dr. Vasant Lad of The Ayurvedic Institute, for illuminating the resonance of the eight limbs of yoga in life's daily dance. No words can fully express my gratitude.

Thank you so much, Mom and Dad, for your love and support—and thank you, ancestors, for lighting the way.

And thank you, dear readers, for being a part of this journey; thank you each for the valuable work you contribute every day in this ongoing journey of life!

Julie Dunlop is a poet, an author, and a teacher of yoga, Āyurveda, and writing. Her book, *Ocean of Yoga: Meditations on Yoga and Āyurveda for Balance, Awareness, and Wellbeing*, was published by Singing Dragon in London in 2017. Dunlop has taught daily yoga classes in the weeklong wellbeing program (*Pañcakarma*) at The Ayurvedic Institute in Albuquerque, NM for five years, and she enjoys sharing pathways to wellbeing with the community through classes and workshops; she is certified through Yoga Alliance (RYT 500, E-RYT 200), the National Ayurvedic Medical Association (CAP), and holds B.A. and M.A. degrees in English. Her previous publications with Finishing Line Press include *Breath, Bone, Earth, Sky* (2014) and *Bending Back the Night* (2012). Dunlop has held writing residencies at Virginia Center for the Creative Arts (VCCA) and Vermont Studio Center (VSC); in 2019, she was a finalist for *Bellevue Literary Review*'s poetry prize, and in 2016, her poetry was awarded the Editor's Prize for Poetry from *Bosque Journal*. Her poetry has been published in a variety of national journals, such as *Journal of the American Medical Association (JAMA), The Threepenny Review, Poet Lore, North Carolina Literary Review, South Dakota Review, Baltimore Review, Potomac Review, Atlanta Review, Harpur Palate, Cold Mountain Review, Appalachian Heritage*, and others. Additionally, her prose has appeared in *Journal of the American Medical Association (JAMA), Ayurveda Journal of Health, Radiologic Technology, Appalachian Heritage*, and *Wake Forest Magazine*. With gratitude, she integrates the ancient wisdom of yoga into her writing, which centers upon the sacred healing at the heart of language and life.

www.ingramcontent.com/pod-product-compliance
Lightning Source LLC
Chambersburg PA
CBHW042142160426
43201CB00022B/2372